Homemade

BIOGRAPHY

ALSO BY TOM ZOELLNER

*The Heartless Stone: A Journey Through the World of
Diamonds, Deceit, and Desire*

AND WITH TOM ZOELLNER
An Ordinary Man: An Autobiography by Paul Rusesabagina

Homemade

BIOGRAPHY

HOW TO COLLECT, RECORD, AND TELL
THE LIFE STORY OF SOMEONE YOU LOVE

TOM ZOELLNER

 St. Martin's Griffin ✠ New York

www.stmartins.com

Design by Nancy Singer Olaguera

Library of Congress Cataloging-in-Publication Data

Zoellner, Tom.
    Homemade biography : how to collect, record, and tell the
    life story of someone you love / Tom Zoellner. — 1st ed.
        p. cm.
    ISBN-13: 978-0-312-34831-1
    ISBN-10: 0-312-34831-2
    1. Biography as a literary form—Study and teaching.   2. Bi-
ography—Study and teaching.   3. Interviewing—Study and
teaching.   4. Family—Research.   I. Title.

CT22 .Z64 2007
809'.93592—dc22

                                                    2007021178

First Edition: October 2007

10 9 8 7 6 5 4 3 2 1

Contents

Foreword

Mildred Baker had just one toy: a red ball with blue and yellow stripes. She played with it daily, rolling it across the floor. She was eight years old and lived on a wheat farm with her aunt and uncle and some cousins outside the small town of Smith Center, Kansas.

The ball was lost one day in 1919. Her uncle Jim had been building an addition onto the house. His carpentry was not precise. There was a crack in the floor, about seven inches wide, where two rooms met each other. Cold air whistled through it in the wintertime. It was just big enough to get a hand through and the opening was dark. Mildred always tried to avoid it, but one day, she lost control of the ball and it rolled into the crack and disappeared into the obscure regions below the house. It was too deep to reach. Her uncle tried to shine a light down the crack, but there was no sign of the ball. It was gone.

Mildred had a tough, impoverished childhood. Drylands farming was a touch-and-go struggle for many families on the plains and Mildred's was no exception. She later said that the only gift her father had been able to give her was an empty tobacco tin. She went on to marry a neighbor boy named Newell Lambert when she was in her late teens. They joined the Thornburg United Methodist Church and had six children. All of the children were born at home, with the help of a midwife. Within her family, Mildred was known for her excellent pancakes and her no-nonsense demeanor, which seemed melancholy at times, almost brooding.

She grew into middle age and beyond. Her sight began to weaken. In 1991, when she was eighty-six years old, she moved with her daughter Sharon into a new house in Smith Center. That was the same year the family decided to tear down the farmhouse where Mildred had grown up, and plow the land underneath it. Mildred told her nephew, Cecil, half-jokingly, "If you find a ball in there, I want it."

On Christmas Day that year, the family gathered at Mildred's new house for dinner. Sharon remembers what it was like in the living room that night:

There were like sixty-one of us in our house in town. That's pretty crowded. But Santa Claus came in and he turned to Mother and he said, "Mildred Lambert, I have a gift for you." And Mom kind of looked at him really surprised, because the adults don't usually get the gifts. He said something like, "Have you been good?" And she kind of laughed and said yes. And she took the gift, and Dad helped her unwrap it some. And the house—you just can't imagine, with [all] of us, small children to the adults—it just got perfectly still, because we all knew what was in that package. And she took it out and she held it in her hand and she looked at it. And she didn't say anything. And somebody asked her, "Mom, what is it?" And she said, "Well, it's a ball." And still the house was very still. And someone said, "Well, Mom, is it an old or a new ball?" And Mom, in a very quiet voice, said, "It's a very old ball."

When Cecil had the old family house torn down, his contractor had indeed discovered Mildred's childhood toy in the wreckage. It had lain under the house for seventy-eight years and was returned to her in the twilight of her life.

You can do something similar.

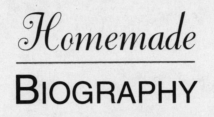

Homemade
BIOGRAPHY

1

Worth Saving

ailure looks like Phoenix. This was the general drift of
my thinking during the spring of 2003, when I moved
back to the southwestern city where I grew up. I didn't particularly want to be there. It was a choice I made after a
string of misfortunes.

Over the course of one eventful month, I had been laid
off from my newspaper job in California and had seen the
disintegration of my engagement to a women I loved. I had
also abandoned the hope of finding a publisher for a short
novel I had written there in my off-hours. I was broke and
unhappy and feeling washed-up, though I was barely out of
my twenties. There was an open spot on the metro desk of
my Arizona hometown newspaper and I accepted it as a way
of getting my life back on track. At least I would be living in
a city where I knew a few old friends, and where the streets
led. But I could not shake the feeling that I had turned out to
be nothing but a disappointment to myself and to everybody
who knew me. I had gone to San Francisco with ambitions,

but I had failed there both as a fiancé and as a novelist. And so it seemed karmically appropriate that I was slinking back to my hometown, a place I had only wanted to escape while I was growing up.

I have complicated feelings about Arizona. I have loved the place and I have hated it, too, both feelings occasionally expressing themselves simultaneously. My hometown of Phoenix, for example, is a real estate agent's fantasy. The metro area spreads like a quilt made of black asphalt, red tile, and Bermuda grass over more than two thousand square miles of desert. The urbanized land mass is equal to that of the Los Angeles basin, the population is greater than that of the Republic of Ireland, and it can take five hours to drive across it when traffic is thick, which it usually is. The main roads are seven-laned, wide as midwestern rivers; most intersections are anchored by twenty-four-hour convenience stores and strip malls. The only natural river is called the Salt and it was dammed dry a century ago to water the cotton fields and orange trees. Heat can rise to 120 degrees in June. Housing promoters called the city "The Valley of the Sun" during the sixties and the name stuck. I grew up in a ranch-style house on the north side of town, off the tee of the eleventh hole of a golf course, and near the slope of a coffin-shaped mound covered with lumps of hardened magma. It was named Moon Mountain and I used to climb it for a view of the golf links and the turquoise dots of swimming pools. When I was a kid, I pretended my bicycle was actually a motorcycle and I dreamed constantly of places beyond the mountains and the golf course and of all the places that I would visit and, possibly, live in. Now I was coming back to Phoenix, and it felt like I was sneaking in through the back door.

I drove into town that March evening with my jeep

loaded to the roof with everything I owned at the time: a few pots and pans, a few books, a backpack, a wristwatch, an old Macintosh computer carefully wrapped in a blanket. It was just after sunset and the last smudges of pink were on the mountains. The air was full of night warmth and the smell of orange blossoms. There was a couch waiting for me at my grandmother's house, in a small adobe-walled house that I had been visiting since I was little. My grandmother had lived there for most of her life. It was where my mother had grown up and where my father had come to pick her up for their first date. There used to be a mailbox out front bearing the words *Lazy B Ranch* written in black paint.

Ours was a relatively old, working-class family in a state overflowing with newcomers. I knew a little bit of the saga: that my great-great-granddad had moved down from Idaho to be a doctor and couldn't get a license from the Arizona Territory to practice medicine and had turned to farming cotton instead. I knew that the lot where my grandmother's house stands had been acquired free of charge as ranchland from the U.S. government under the Homestead Act of 1862. It had once been a part of a much larger parcel of desert that had been sold off in the Depression and is now part of a golf-and-tennis resort (a not uncommon fate for land in metro Phoenix). But my knowledge ended there.

I pulled into the dirt driveway on Mockingbird Lane that night, kissed Grandma hello on top of her gray hair, and settled in to stay a week or two until I could find a place of my own to rent. When she asked me how I was doing, I only smiled and told her I was fine. She poured a glass of supermarket box wine and we toasted each other and then turned toward the television.

It may have been that first night, or some night shortly

thereafter, but at some point that week, I said over my wine-glass: "Hey, tell me that story again. About the guy who owned the water company."

"You mean, Mr. Cheney?"

"Yes. Didn't you tell me he had some kind of scam in the 1940s where he bought up one inch of all the properties that faced the street?"

"Why, yes. He said he had bought a long strip of land one foot wide that ran for more than a mile and threatened to charge people an easement fee for crossing onto their own property from the street. Their own property! He even put up a barbed-wire fence on his one-foot strip and ran it all the way down Mockingbird Lane. We used to carry wire cutters in the car and just cut the damn thing open whenever we came back to the house."

I have always enjoyed hearing this story—and, I have to say, I was amused by the irritation she still felt about it sixty years later. I realized that I must have made her tell it at least three times over the past few years. But I could never quite recall all the details. *I really ought to write this down*, I thought. *She's not going to be around forever*. But I did nothing about it at that point.

My grandmother has been in my life, of course, since I was a baby, but until that moment I couldn't say that I really knew much that was substantial about her, or that we were "close" in any meaningful way, other than the artificial closeness of people who happen to be related by blood but don't spend much time together. I knew that her career had been spent as a civil service secretary, mostly for various state agencies. There was a framed certificate of thanks on her wall, signed by the governor and presented to her upon retirement. I saw her at Christmas and Easter and we always exchanged pleasantries. She had been very forgiving when I was twelve and accidentally broke a margarita glass at her house and tried to hide the evidence. She made excellent tacos. On every birthday, a Hallmark card arrived with a crisp five-dollar bill inside. But she was an elderly woman who did crossword puzzles for fun and I was an awkward, unruly boy who wanted to play in the NBA; we didn't seem to have a lot to talk about when I was growing up. Since I had grown older, the talk had become more genuine—about politics, Arizona history, that water company scam—but I still couldn't claim to know much about her as a person that spring when I moved back to Phoenix. She was then eighty-seven years old.

I settled into my newspaper job and rented a brick house a few miles away. But I kept coming back to Grandma's. We started having dinner every Monday night. It was one reliable weekly event in what was turning out to be a long, low period for me. And it was a relief to be there, where I didn't have to think about my own situation. At these dinners, we talked more and more about the life she had lived and the things that she had seen.

There was a basket of surprises. I learned that Vern, her first husband and my biological grandfather, had been a serious commitment-phobe and had married and divorced eight women before he died (Grandma had been wife number three). I learned that an uncle of mine had been a heroin addict back in the 1950s. A cousin had gone to prison for burglary. I heard about her first job as a New Deal–era clerk in a government warehouse in Tucson, and relatives of whom I had been only dimly aware took on sharper identities and personalities. I began to look forward to these dinners and never let plans with anyone else get in the way.

Then came the day in autumn when Grandma took a bad fall getting out of the car. I wasn't there at the time. Her face was covered with bruises, and her embarrassment was acute, but she was otherwise unhurt. It still put a shock into me. And several thoughts coalesced very quickly.

One was: *I spend all day interviewing people and then writing stories. What's stopping me from writing down Grandma's story?*

Another was sad and troubling. I had been spending a lot of time that year wondering if I would ever be married or be a father. *She may never get to see any children I might have. And they may never know her.*

A last one was simply this: *I don't ever want to forget her.*

The following Monday, I showed up with a tape recorder.

"I want to get the story of your life down on paper," I told her. "Would you be willing?"

That was the start of one of the best things I've ever done.

"Civilization is a stream with banks," said the historian Will Durant. "The stream is sometimes filled with blood from people killing, stealing, shouting, and doing things historians usually record—while, on the banks, unnoticed, people build homes, make love, whittle statues. The story of civilization is the story of what happens on the banks."

This book is about the people who lived on the side of the river, the ones who never ran for elective office, made a scientific discovery, played in a World Series, built a dam, gave a speech, or otherwise attracted attention beyond their neighborhood, but whose lives still counted for something.

They mattered. Ordinary people built the world with trillions of acts of obscure heroism lost to common memory. There were armies of these now-forgotten people. They grew trees, passed minor laws, sold bread, taught correct spelling, raised polite children. They knew familiar experiences common to all: the taste of good food, the smell of a rainy morning, the touch of another person. Publicity and luck may have secured visited grave sites for a select few, but both the famous and the forgotten have stories that ought to be preserved.

What we call *history* is, above all, the story of those countless people: what they saw, how they acted, what they built, who they married, why they took the right turn instead of the left, who paid their salary and picked their pocket and how they felt about the whole baffling mess at the end of the day.

The stories of our parents and grandparents are the ones most primary to us; they leave their tracings within us; they gave us the color of our hair and the shape of our tempers, they move with us in our muscles and eyes. Stories of the old ones, passed down through spoken word, have provided a backbone to almost every culture on earth. There may be no more emblematic figure of what we call "civilization" than the lone man standing before a village assembly, relating a tale of what he had seen over the mountain ridge or singing a song about the warriors he had slain or calling out a list of his distinguished ancestors. This is a feature of every civilization. The heroic Greek epics were meant to be recited from memory. The Gospel author Luke says that he personally investigated the stories of Jesus "as they were handed down to us" by eyewitnesses. Likewise, children in Somalia are expected to recite their own genealogy going back twenty generations in order to prove their ties to the larger society.

The classic expression of history—that of scientists and kings and troop movements—tends to ignore the experiences of ordinary people, but some writers have always known that the genuine marrow of life does not always reveal itself at the base of the throne or wherever gunpowder flashes. The most celebrated and widely read history of France was published in 1867 by Jules Michelet, who spent a significant amount of his research time not in the libraries, but recording the opinions and experiences of peasants and workingmen all across the nation. In Britain at roughly the same period, Thomas Macaulay partly drew on ballads and barroom tales to complete his *History of England*. "The only true history of a country," he once said, "is to be found in its newspapers." In the United States, the writer Studs Terkel has made a career of recording the stories of janitors, mechanics, bums, schoolteachers, bankers, and people from every imaginable background to create a tapestry of American history made up of a thousand different experiences and impressions.

The simple fact of being alive and conscious with a brain as powerful as that of a human being—"the wet computer," as some biologists call it—is enough to make just about anybody interesting by sheer default. They have loved and suffered and questioned and fought the maddening ambiguity of life, just as we have.

But how well do we know some of those who have been beside us all this time?

After dinner on Monday nights, my grandmother and I would go into the living room. She would sit on the couch and I would sit in a side chair. We drank more supermarket wine. And the reels on the tape recorder spun.

I learned that Grandma had walked to high school each day by going east from her house on Polk Street over to the far side of downtown. This would seem to be a trivial detail of geography, but it meant something to me. I had just moved to an apartment half a mile from the newspaper's office and had gotten into the habit of walking to work on the days when the heat wasn't too oppressive. My daily path led south, through the heart of downtown. So twice each day, at some point on the sidewalk, I was stepping over the route that my Grandma took seventy years earlier. This pleased me enormously. I lived in a different kind of Phoenix than she had known, dirtier and shabbier, perhaps, but it was still the same city and the streets still had the same names.

My apartment was also not far from the old Greek-columned elementary school building, now abandoned, where she had been given crayons to draw pictures in kindergarten. "I loved the orange ones," she told me. "I always went for the orange and the poor kindergarten class never had any orange ones because I used them all up. Whatever I colored, it was orange." The crayons had smelled bitter, "an odor I can still remember, a nice waxy smell." I know that scent myself. Who doesn't?

In the fifth week, she told me about the marriage to her first husband, Vern. He had proposed to her at a restaurant near the capitol at lunchtime one day in 1941 and she "floated" back to her secretarial job at the Highway Department with a ring to show all the girls. They were married less than a month later in a quickie wedding chapel in Las Vegas because the divorce from his second wife was not yet official in Arizona. My mother was born not long after, but the marriage was not a good one. Vern loved to go out and drink and be raucous at the downtown bars. My grandmother enjoyed the large life at first, but began to crave nights at home and playing cards and other quiet activities she thought were more suited to domesticity. When they fought, Vern would never stick around to talk things over. His habit, she said, was to storm off to his mother's house. Then he would feel guilty and send flowers. "So I accumulated a lot of flowers," she said. More suspiciously, Vern took up bowling as a new hobby and would go by himself to the lanes downtown. Grandma never went along. She suspected it was a cover to go chase girls. He did nothing to clear up this impression, even after coming home with lipstick smears on his shirt. Their breakup seemed inevitable, and indeed he asked her for a divorce after he took up with a woman he said he met while out "bowling."

Their seven-year marriage quickly unraveled. The divorce proceedings were efficient: He took the car, she claimed the house where they lived on Virginia Street. In the summer of 1948, my grandma was left with no steady job, no car, and a baby daughter to raise by herself. She took my mother to day care on the city bus every morning. Both her parents were dead. Friends were scarce. She didn't know where to go for comfort. For my grandma in that unhappy season of her life, failure looked a lot like Phoenix.

"Just as you feel when you look on the river or sky, so I felt," said the great American poet Walt Whitman in "Crossing Brooklyn Ferry." "I too walked the streets of Manhattan island and bathed in the waters around it. I too felt the curious abrupt questionings stir in me."

Taking down a history of one of your relatives is rewarding in ways you may not have counted upon. It brings the generations closer together. It reminds older people that their lives were interesting and worthwhile. It creates a record of a life that goes far deeper than names and dates on a family tree.

Most of all, it engenders one of the noblest and best states available to humanity: that of empathy. This is an idea I will keep returning to in the course of this book. Empathy conquers selfishness. It conquers loneliness. It is what makes civilization possible, and what makes love inevitable. It is a good tool for any writer to have, and one that cannot be forced or faked. But I guarantee that if you embark on this project with an open mind, it will emerge naturally and almost effortlessly.

The stream of our private thoughts rolls by unseen by the rest of the world. But the strangeness of that inner life would surely be recognizable and unsurprising to most anyone who could see inside. These stories you'll take down can be read and appreciated by people who don't know us and who may never know us except through what we leave on the pages for them to discover fifty or a hundred or five hundred years from today. I'm not sure who might be reading about my grandmother, Ann Mary von Blume, in the future, but the document is there. It is not the most beautifully written story ever penned, but names and addresses and dates and all other kinds of things that I surely would have forgotten are now down on the page. The entire project took ten weeks. I collected about fifteen hours' worth of tape. I asked questions of my grandmother in an easygoing interviewing style that I had learned as a newspaper reporter and which I'll discuss in this book. I turned audiotape into instant prose using an easy method I'll also describe in a later chapter.

It would be too simple to say that doing this project was responsible for leading me out of the doldrums—though that eventually happened—but I know that becoming closer to my grandma during that time in Phoenix was a gift, and one I might not have had if I hadn't started asking questions and discovering that the person across the Thanksgiving table all those years was a thoroughly complex and multilayered person, just as I was. Just as we all are.

In writing a Homemade Biography, you will be committing an act of deep selflessness. When you and I and everyone we know are gone and dust, this careful reckoning of a life will remain in a bank vault or a basement or a trunk in an attic, to be discovered by somebody we can still touch with our words and make them see what was important to us. It will tell anybody who cares to look into those pages that the life documented within them was worth living. It is a shout across the ages: *I existed.*

And the larger lesson is this: *Reader, your life is worth living, too.*

CASE STUDY

Unexpected Results

When Ted Kearsley set out to interview his cousin, he knew he had a difficult task in front of him.

The cousin, William Thompson, lived in a hand-built house on the edge of a swamp in Farmingdale, New York. He had grown up in the segregated South, drove firetrucks on the front lines during

World War II, and played in the Negro baseball leagues before Jackie Robinson broke the color barrier. In addition to being an interesting man in his own right, William was an indispensable link in the family's sense of its own history. William had interviewed an uncle in 1946, and had also had several conversations in the 1920s with Ted's great-great-grandmother Amanda, who had been raised as a slave in a Confederate household in the area near the Appomattox River in Virginia.

But William was regarded by the rest of the family as somewhat eccentric. He always recited Bible verses, for one thing, and had a habit of talking about other people as if they were more religious and devout than they really were. Such behavior was, perhaps, William's own way of reassuring himself that everyone in the family knew the peace of Christianity as he did himself. Ted, however, was raised a Methodist in a more staid religious culture and William's Pentecostal eruptions often left him confused.

So when Ted went out to Farmingdale with a tape recorder, he knew the conversation would probably be a long one, and he resolved not to get impatient. It turned out to be the best thing he could have done.

"You can never show a desire to leave," says Ted. "People can tell when you're acting impatient or checking your watch. You just have to let the story come out at its own speed."

By staying mainly silent, Ted found himself able to coax stories out of William without too many digressions. It helped him greatly that he had seen a negative example of how *not* to handle William. Another relative had recently come in with a tape recorder and a list of structured, point-by-point questions from which she refused to diverge. She constantly interrupted William and made him feel like he was being interrogated rather than drawn out. And so, not surprisingly, William closed down and the conversation yielded little of value.

Ted's technique was simple. He came in not with a list of questions, but a diagrammed tree of the family's Virginia branch. Ted would simply read off a name he recollected from his childhood and the stories started coming. This is one of the great advantages any family member has when interviewing another—the shared remembrance of people. It can create a sense of experience common to both, which leads to a better conversation and a better interview.

Ted had another point of commonality with William: the experience of being associated with the army and of the military mindset. Ted had worked for years as a counselor and instructor at a Veteran's Administration hospital in upstate New York and William had fought in the Battle of the Bulge in World War II. Ted understood the subtleties of conversations about war; he knew when to coax and when to listen. When he felt it was appropriate, he said, he would mention his own experiences with the military just so that William knew he was talking with a peer.

These points of shared experience are invaluable when speaking with a person about their adult experiences. Whether it be frustrations with work, the dramas of dating, the challenges of marriage and raising children, the thrill of buying a first house, or anything else, these moments when two people discover a point of agreement or kinship on a subject are like little explosions of gasoline inside a cylinder. They push the conversation forward. The key, of course, is to use this fuel *only* to get the other person to talk about themselves. Don't flood the engine by talking too much about yourself.

William's recollections were drenched with Biblical references and with possible pseudohistory, (i.e., painting certain relatives as superdevout when their faith may have been only lukewarm), but at the very least they served to let William express himself as he really was. To have censored his spiritual life out of his biography would have been a crime against William, and would have stripped him of his humanity to anyone in the family who wanted to read about him years later.

"Our family played on God's team," William liked to say, "but our names were never in the Hall of Fame at Cooperstown."

William died in 1995 in a nursing home in Queens, but he left behind a six-page document, painstakingly written in an arthritic hand, telling the story of his own life. A fascinating passage occurs about halfway through in which he describes being stationed at an army post in central New Jersey in 1943, just before his company was sent overseas.

"I had the opportunity to go to Atlantic City twice," he wrote. "I attended the Catholic morning service, and also attended the Methodist service twice. Here I met a young Christian lady who showed very much an interest in myself. She worked at the place where the government had set up areas for the soldiers to gather or rooms if they wanted to stay overnight. I never got the chance but to see her once again. Other soldiers told me in my company that she had asked about me."

Readers think, *aha,* now there's the woman who will later go on to be his wife. But we're in for a surprise. William instead married a lady named Wilhelmina after the war and we never see this young Christian lady from the honky-tonk beach town again. That this fleeting encounter would emerge in the mind of an elderly man in a nursing home in Queens fifty years later seems to be worthy of some elaboration. She lives today only on paper.

I asked Ted if his cousin ever mentioned the mystery woman again and he e-mailed me the following response.

William never mentioned that lady in any of our conversations. I think that some people that you meet over a lifetime leave a lasting impression and you wonder what might have been. I recall young ladies that I met in the forties that I shall never forget. Being in the service you usually move on and never see them again. However, I guess I was luckier than William because two of them that I met in 1946 got in touch with me fairly recently.

Ted

PS—They really are a nuisance . . .

2

The First Session

Your first task will be to persuade your grandfather, grandmother, uncle, aunt, parent, or whomever to allow their lives to be documented. In almost every case, this should be easy. Many people, particularly the elderly, yearn for nothing more than a respectful listener. They might make a halfhearted attempt to wave you off, or pretend to be grumpy about it, but most will feel the glow of gratitude inside.

In cases where some persuasion is required, try making one or more of the following appeals. You are the most qualified to tell which one of them might spark the interest of a reluctant subject:

- "I know that your life has had a lot of interesting elements. I want to hear about them."
- "You always have such good stories. I want to get them down right so I can always remember the details."

- "We don't have to talk about anything you'd rather not address." (Keep this promise, too.)
- "I want my own grandchildren to have a sense of who you are/were." (Use your best judgment on whether to use the past tense or the present.)
- "I feel like I know you pretty well, but I always feel like there's more I want to know."
- "I've never understood this one particular aspect of your life."
- "Today's world is so different from yesterday's. I want to understand more about what life was like back then."
- "They say those who don't learn from history are doomed to repeat it. I want to know what not to do."
- "Come on—it'll be fun to remember all this stuff again! Give it a try for just an hour and if you're annoyed, we'll stop." (Your last-ditch pitch.)

THE MIDDLE SPACE

A number of things are going to happen the first time you have a Homemade Biography conversation. One of the most important is that you'll help set the tone for every session that follows.

Every exchange between two people contains a hidden life: an unconscious process of finding each other's rhythm and adjusting our own pose accordingly. This "middle space" is unique to the relationship. It's like a diaphanous balloon that encompasses both of you. With some people, you share atmospheres that are large and full of light and color; with others, you breathe inside a stuffy and cheerless tent. An average life sees billions of these spaces, forming and reforming as we end conversations and start new ones.

Each of our relationships is defined by the quality of the middle space.

In undertaking this project, you're going to want that space to be full of curiosity and respect. In your first session, the key is to set a tone that promotes good feelings between you and your subject. Here are a few ideas for setting the right mood:

- Make an appointment ahead of time. Don't get down to business immediately.
- Dress nicely, but not churchy.
- If you don't live in the same house, go over to where they live. People always feel more comfortable in their own dwellings.
- Get a quiet room away from house traffic. Choose the living room over the family room.
- Sit close, but not *too* close. The ideal is to have the subject in an easy chair and you on the couch, facing them.
- Have a few beverages on hand to sip together. If you're the drinking sort, have *one* glass of wine or beer.
- Chat about inconsequential things for a few minutes. Enjoy each other's company.

THE TIMELINE

What you *don't* want to do in this first session is flip on the tape recorder and say, "So . . . tell me about your life." In fact, you may want to consider leaving the tape recorder at home for now (more on this later). The only tools you really need at this point are a pencil and an ordinary legal pad.

Tell the subject you want to make a timeline so you won't get confused later on. This tool is critical. The dates and locations of another's life easily become jumbled for anyone who didn't live through it, and many interview subjects tend to forget this. You'll be saving yourself an enormous amount of trouble later on (and also sparing your subject some distracting interruptions down the road: "Now wait a minute, did this happen when you were living in Spokane and married to Amy, or in Minneapolis and married to Glenda?").

Start by getting the subject's birth date and year and note it in the upper left corner of the legal pad. Let's say it's April 24, 1938. Each line of your legal pad after that represents a year in your subject's life, leading up to the present. To keep the chronology straight for yourself at a glance, count two lines down and write "1940" on the left side. Count another ten and write "1950," and so on, up to the present year.

Remind the subject that this is only an organizing tool and the real questions are to follow. Don't give them the impression that this is the whole game, as the questions you'll be asking here are of the most superficial variety. What you want them to do is walk you quickly through the bare bones of their life story—places, people, dates. Find out when she moved from her girlhood home on the farm into suburban Chicago. When was her brother born? When did her dad die? When did she marry Bob? Write the dates of these significant life events—either approximate or exact—on the left-hand side of the page with some brief commentary on the right. If she's moved from house to house, get the addresses. If he's jumped from job to job, get the names of the companies.

Building this timeline accomplishes many things at once. It eases you gently into somebody's life story in a nonthreatening way. It conveys your desire to get things right and boosts your credibility. And, of course, it will save you a lot of confusion down the road when the conversation takes leave of plain fact and gets more involved with emotional truths.

By the time your timeline creeps into your subject's middle age, your legal pad will probably be quite messy, full of cross-outs and erasures. That's okay. You'll clean it up later. For now the important part is getting a working chronology of the person's trajectory through life—not just on paper but in your mind.

It's likely this initial conversation will go off on a few tangents, and that's okay, too. The subject will probably have a few interesting qualitative things to say about that marriage to Bob or that decision to buy the furniture store. Listen and enjoy, but feel no compulsion to write it all down. Just remember to come back to it in a future session. You could make a brief note of it on the timeline next to an asterisk (i.e., *—ask about the robbery*). Keep the timeline moving forward. During especially busy years in their life, the lines may get crowded with entries. You could handle this in one of two ways. You could draw lines to a circled "balloon" of information placed among the uneventfulness of quieter years. Or you could improvise a footnote system by drawing a big letter of the alphabet when you run out of room. Then flip to a blank page in your legal pad and note the stuff that's keyed to A or B or C, and so on.

Once you've made it to the present year, you're all done. Take a last look at your timeline and make sure nothing in it confuses you. And be sure to remind the subject that much more is to come; that this simple walk through the milestones of life is only a prelude to the real biography. Have another drink and relax.

Later that day or the next, you should clean up this timeline while the conversation is still fresh in your mind.

Either copy it down in neat order on another page, or—if, like mine, your handwriting is sloppy—use a word processor to organize the key dates and names into a document that can serve as an easy reference tool. Ideally it should fit on just one or two pages of paper. You're going to want to take it with you to every session that follows so you'll be able to keep track of events in a monologue that may wander over the years.

Perhaps the best reason of all to start the project with a timeline is that it provides a gentle point of entry for both of you. People who might be intimidated with the prospect of a freewheeling discussion about their lives will find it easy and nonthreatening to walk you through the high points. You don't need to ask any hard questions. They don't need to feel embarrassed. They can see what you're doing, right there on plain paper. It gives you time to get used to each other's voices, and to work together on something concrete.

End this visit by asking for a future conversation. See if they'll agree to a weekly session, every Monday evening, for example. Tell them you want to go into much greater detail about the interesting aspects of their childhoods, their parents, their jobs, and their experiences. If it's appropriate, offer to cook dinner or bring food and a bottle of wine. My suggestion is to put the date on the calendar right then and there: You don't want it to be forgotten.

TO TAPE OR NOT TO TAPE

This is a minor issue, thankfully, but one you'll have to confront nonetheless. Should you tape this first session? There's no right answer, unfortunately, only advantages and disadvantages. My approach with my grandmother was to start taping her immediately, but you may be better off easing the recorder into the mix after you've both gotten comfortable with each other.

The tape recorder, for many people, is an off-putting object. The black box makes many people feel they ought to choose their words carefully because they could come back to haunt them. It can lend a feeling of interrogation to a conversation that should be casual and free. And because this first session will be so anchored to simple names and dates instead of complex thoughts, you may wish to leave the tape recorder at home. The job of extracting oral history is always a subconscious tango between the subject and the interviewer, each feeling out the other's conversational styles. There may be no need to introduce the distraction of the recorder at this stage. You should be able to get down the timeline easily enough with just pen and paper. I taped conversations only occasionally when I was a newspaper reporter; the deadlines were always too near and the conversations were usually too short to justify the hassle.

Depending on the personality of your subject, this might be the right time to unapologetically pull out the recorder. Your subject might be the kind of person who would appreciate your desire to get things down exactly and correctly. They may also enjoy seeing that their words are considered important enough to commit to tape. And unless you are a genius with stenography, or can write *extremely* fast, the tape recorder is an indispensable tool in a Homemade Biography. It will likely have to emerge at some point, and perhaps this first session is the best time to get your subject comfortable with it.

I wish I could give you a clear-cut answer here. But instead, I have to defer to you, the reader, as the best possible judge of what will work well in your situation. Nobody is better equipped than you to decide what would sit best in your subject's living room.

At whatever point the recorder comes out—and I recommend you never attempt a biography without one—your number-one goal will be to make the subject forget about it as soon as possible. You want them speaking directly to you, another human being, and not the device.

You can help set the right tone by not making a big production out of the thing. Stand the recorder in a place where it can easily pick up both your voices, but avoid looking at it. Make a few jokes as it starts to run. Keep eye contact. Speak in a light and careless voice. If you treat the recorder as no big deal, your subject can't help but unconsciously follow your lead. In most cases, they'll be unaware of its presence within ten minutes.

This should go without saying: Don't ever tape a person without their knowledge. If they insist on eschewing the recorder altogether, you might try making the case that you are committed to getting everything down verbatim and the tape is essential for that. You might also consider saying that you enjoy the sound of their voice and want to remember it years from now, or that you want to play it for your own grandchildren someday.

A WORD ON TECHNOLOGY

When I started taping my grandmother, I used an ordinary cassette recorder powered with AA batteries. This one was purchased from RadioShack for about $40. It had a frame of black plastic and took microcassettes barely an inch and a half long that could record an hour of conversation on each side. It was light, and easy to carry in a coat pocket because it was only about as big as two packs of cigarettes. The sound quality was mediocre, but I could make out the conversation if I turned the volume all the way up. I would have had less background noise if I had used the kind of bulky tape recorders that have been around since the 1970s and are still used by some radio reporters today. They're slightly cheaper than the microcassette recorders and they take standard-sized tapes, but they're heavier, and about the size of a shaving kit.

Because the ultimate point of these interviews is to preserve your subject's recollections far into the future, I would recommend investing in a digital tape recorder and then converting the interviews to an MP3 or WAVE file. Your subject's voice can then be saved on your computer's hard drive and on as many compact discs as you choose to burn. They will have a better chance of surviving a century inside an attic trunk than cassette tapes, which are made of ferric oxide and cobalt and may be subject to crumbling and stretching. I feel quite sure that compact discs will themselves become obsolete before too long—in the same way that cassette tapes are now fading away—but I also feel certain that the technology wizards of the next century will be able to retrieve the audio from either medium without too much trouble.

As of this writing, a small digital recorder can be purchased for anywhere from $75 to $200, and can save between five hours and two hundred hours of conversation, depending on the size of its memory chip. You can then transfer the contents to your computer using a standard USB cable. The disadvantage, however, is that you can't just pop in a new cassette tape if you run out of room. You'll have to download the whole thing to your computer before proceeding anew.

Let's say you decide to go the old-fashioned route and use audiotape. Or let's say you recorded some conversations before the advent of digital technology. Is there a way to transfer them to compact disc? Happily, there is, and it is a very easy process. You will need a tape deck and also a computer that has a sound card with an exterior port labeled LINE IN, which should be colored baby blue. Go to your local electronics store and ask the clerk for a stereo RCA cable, sometimes called a "Y connector," as well as a mini jack. Hook up a pair of twin connectors to the two stereo tape deck female receptors labeled LINE OUT, plug the other two into the mini jack, insert the single male end of the mini jack into the LINE IN port on your computer, boot up your music program, hit PLAY on your tape deck, and start recording. It's that simple. I would recommend this as a method of preserving the conversations on the computer, even if you plan to write your biography from the audiotapes.

A basic, but crucial, note about taping in either format. *Make sure you are actually recording the conversation!* I have come away from more than one interview with a useless tape because I failed to take basic precautions. First of all, make sure your batteries are fresh. Glance at the recorder every ten minutes or so to make sure the wheels are still turning, or that the digital face is still lit up. Make sure the buttons on the recorder aren't set to PAUSE or VOICE ACTIVATED or PHONE or another setting that prohibits the continuous recording of sound in a room. And, most important of all, test the acoustics of the room before you start the interview. Put your recorder on the table in the room where you plan to be speaking, set it to RECORD, speak a few words in a low-to-normal voice, and play it back to see how it sounds.

You might be surprised at what you hear. The air conditioner that seems barely audible to naked ears can sound like a Florida hurricane on tape. Same goes for any other kind of ambient noise, which may turn into a roar upon replay and could easily ruin hours of recorded conversation. You won't want to ask your subject to tell a story a second time: It's never quite the same.

OTHERS IN THE ROOM

Your project will probably attract some interest within the family, and those people who live in the same house with your subject will be curious and may plunk themselves down uninvited to listen to the stories. There will be times when you would want another participant in the discussion (more on this in a later chapter), but certainly not for the whole life saga. Generally speaking, you're better off keeping this conversation limited to two people.

The presence of a third person—particularly a family member with their own opinions on a historical matter—will inevitably change the tone and content of your subject's memories. Your chances of hearing them speak with candor about a sensitive topic will likely diminish, for one thing. The subject may be afraid to disclose something important out of fear of offending or confusing the new listener. They may also feel subtle pressure to keep their stories brief for the sake of not boring an audience. Aunt Jean or Uncle Bob might also feel compelled to insert their own memories into the conversation, which can be interesting, but is ultimately a distraction from the real mission of your project. This is a biography of an individual, not of a group. Even if they don't start chatterboxing, your guests may well grow impatient and start stirring and coughing, thus making your subject anxious to finish up in time for dinner or bedtime—precisely the kind of pressure you do not want stultifying the middle space.

This isn't to say that having a third person around is always a negative experience. They might help prompt some memories—a forgotten name, or a misremembered detail. Their interjections might trigger an unexpected story. They can be great comic relief. They might even be your allies if the subject suddenly gets gun-shy. You won't necessarily get a bad conversation. But you will certainly get a different conversation.

Diplomacy within families is always a tricky (and highly individualized) business. As I said before, you will be the best authority on how to ask Aunt Jean and Uncle Bob to let you have time alone with your subject. You might try scheduling your visits when you know they won't be around. You might try saying: "I really don't want to put Grandpa on the spot in front of too many people" or "He'll talk more comfortably with fewer people in the room" or "We need to get his uninterrupted thoughts." You might ask your subject to do the shooing himself. As a last resort, you might politely say, "Let's let Grandpa tell how it was," if the interruptions get too frequent.

None of this may be feasible, of course. You might just have to accept the gallery seating. But by all means, try to avoid witnessing a performance when you should be having a conversation.

A FINAL THOUGHT ON THE FIRST SESSION

If your experience is typical, this project is going to be a remarkable trip for both of you. It will bring peace and satisfaction to the subject, and open up new windows of understanding for you—about the other person, about yourself, and about the mysteries of life itself.

But don't expect all these things to happen in one evening. You can't force it. It will come with time. Have fun, forget the clock, and lose yourself in the stories.

CASE STUDY

An Alternative Method

Brad Tyer didn't have an idea of how to start talking to his grandmother about her life. So on the first day of his visit to her house in Tyler, Texas, he did the first thing that came to mind—he pulled down one of her photo albums and asked her to point out all the different people in the pictures.

THE TOOLS YOU'LL NEED

If you're not keen on gadgets, here's some good news: A biography is basically a low-tech enterprise. Here is a list of everything you might need to tell a life story.

- A few pens
- Notebook
- Computer with a printer (or a typewriter)
- Tape recorder or digital recorder
- Camcorder (optional; see chapter 9)

"It had occurred to me that if she dies, nobody will know the *names* of these people," he said. "So I turned on the tape recorder and we started flipping through the album."

This strategy for the first session is not necessarily the one I recommend. But it worked beautifully in this case. The photos seemed to have an unlocking effect on the normally shy eighty-four-year-old Dorothy Tyer. She talked for hours about the various people in her life, and it helped create a mood of trust between them.

Specifically, Dorothy needed to trust that Brad was genuinely interested in what she had to say.

"She comes from a long tradition of what people in East Texas call 'poor-mouthing,'" said Brad. "You up-talk your troubles and down-talk your successes. If you've taken in a bumper crop, you're expected to say, 'Man, I'm just barely getting by.' Nobody ever wants to be seen as bragging. And so Dorothy kept saying to me, 'I can't believe you're interested in all of this stuff,' and I had to keep showing her that I really was. The photos were a great place to focus our attentions. I had no idea what I was doing when I pulled down that album, but it turned out to be accidentally brilliant."

The problem with this method, of course, is that it skips around in time. If later on, you attempt to build a narrative out of your material, it can lead to a confusion of dates, times, and places. But that was not Brad's immediate goal. He only wanted to get the stories flowing.

This approach led to a conversation that would not have happened if Brad had been using a more structured method. Dorothy had turned to a photo of a group of men crouching together on the lawn and pointed out one in particular on the photo's edge.

"Oh, that's Eddie C.," she said.

It rang a bell in Brad's mind. He recalled that his father had a running joke with his brothers through the years that Brad had never understood. If somebody was wearing a loud pair of pants, they'd say, "Oh, those are Eddie C. pants." Other oddball choices in fashion or mannerism were also branded as "Eddie C."

"Who was Eddie C.?" Brad asked.

"He was a friend of the family's," said Dorothy. "Everybody liked him, but he was a little different."

"What do you mean different?"

Dorothy squirmed a bit before saying, "He was, you know . . . *that way*," but Brad had already guessed that Eddie was a gay man who could not have been open about his sexual orientation in 1950s Texas.

Brad talked with his grandmother about Eddie being gay for a while. And then she said something that stunned him.

"You know, your father came to me after he divorced your mother and we had a really interesting conversation. He told me he was wondering about the reasons why his marriage had ended and he was contemplating the possibility that he had been gay himself."

Brad's father, aged forty-five at the time, came to the conclusion that he was not gay and kept looking for explanations for his divorce. It was a fascinating detail of family history that Brad had never known, and one that made him see his late father in a new light. This new information didn't make him love or respect his father any less. It only humanized him more. His father had been carrying around a set of thoughts more complex than Brad could have known.

This story highlights one possible method of beginning a first session, but it also speaks to one of the many ways that a Homemade Biography can change the way you think about life. You'll learn surprising things about people you thought you already understood. It can be extremely easy to forget that a family member we've seen across the Thanksgiving dinner table year after year has passed through the world with the same private dramas, passions, failings, horrors, joys, and yearnings as ourselves. Nobody is all that different, in the end. Yet it still fascinates us—and always will—to find the unexpected embedded within the familiar.

So proceed with care. But by all means proceed.

3

Interview Techniques

I once had the privilege of helping a good man write his life story. His name was Paul Rusesabagina and he had been the manager of a hotel in the African nation of Rwanda. In the spring of 1994, a campaign of mass murder broke out against a certain ethnic group, the Tutsis, in Paul's home country and he risked his own life to hide more than a thousand innocent people inside the walls of his hotel. He had saved them through his friendships with some of the military leaders who had planned the genocide. Paul flattered these men shamelessly, drank beers with them, and bribed them with his stock of dwindling cash—all in the name of keeping the refugees under his protection safe from the machetes. Against long odds, Paul survived to tell the tale, and the movie *Hotel Rwanda* was made about his experience.

When Paul invited me to help him write his autobiography, I knew almost nothing about Rwanda, except that it had a magical-sounding name and had been the site of a terrible slaughter. There was an immediate rapport between

Paul and me, and we have since become friends, but I felt exceptionally ignorant in my early conversations with him. He came from a different side of the planet and knew about things I could never imagine. His father raised bananas for a living; mine worked in a bank. He had grown up very poor on a steep hillside in the backcountry of Africa; I had never gone for want of much in my suburban upbringing on the edge of a golf course in Phoenix. He knew what it was like to live every day in fear; my own life, by comparison, had been a model of comfort and peace. He had managed a luxury hotel; I had once stayed in one. On the surface, we had almost nothing in common except a quiet personality and the ability to speak English. This was our starting point.

We knew our roles. My job was to listen and his job was to talk. But it took us awhile to find a rhythm. Our first conversations were about the dominant theme of the book: the Rwandan genocide and what Paul had done in his limited role as a hotel manager to save more than a thousand lives. It was a story he had told many times and in various ways over the years, and much of the raw and messy detail that make for vivid journalism had grown stale with time and worn smooth from repeated tellings. Paul had an excellent memory for dates, a keen sense of political drama, and a manager's attention to correct spellings of names and places, but he had a harder time recounting the little scraps of ordinary life in Rwanda that would make the book really come alive.

We didn't find the key until we started talking about his childhood. I can't remember the conversation exactly, but it went approximately like this: I recall asking him what he remembered of his father. He offered a description of a decent and wise man who was an elder in the local justice court system. Anything else? "Well," said Paul, "he never once raised his voice when I was around. He also never fought with my mother."

This wasn't bad stuff, but it also gave no hint of the true personality of the banana farmer who had had a profound impact on Paul's upbringing. I wasn't sure how to find an opening. There had to be a way of bringing his father to life; he could not be just a cardboard cutout of a man. People may be decent and wise—they often are—but they are never *only* that.

I thought of my own father. How would I describe him to a stranger? He was bald from a young age, about average height, brown eyes. A good listener. Solicitous to older people. Stingy with his money. Loving toward his wife. All of these descriptions are true. But an odd thing comes to mind when I think of the way my father acted when his defenses were down and he was somewhat irate. I have an image of him from my childhood: his eyes narrowed, his cheeks slightly red, his flat midwestern accent spooling out in a rasp when he was cheesed off about something or another: "Welllll, *shit*, Joanne!"

Joanne, of course, was my mother. And although they griped at each other from time to time in front of the kids, we always knew it was the kind of bickering that never leads to bloodletting; almost playful, the cranky jousting of two people who obviously loved each other and felt free to grouse to each other once in a while. There was irritation in his grousing, but also genuine affection for her—as strange as that sounds. When I think of the long-lasting glue between my mom and dad, I recall that old ridiculous kitchen cuss. That memory is one of many keys in my understanding of my father as an individual (which hasn't come easy over the years) and it makes me smile a little when I think of it.

I plunged ahead and asked Paul, "Did your father have

any favorite sayings? You know, things he said over and over that you kind of liked?"

"Oh yes," said Paul. "There was one in particular he told me over and over. 'You never invite a man without a beer.'"

"Beer? You mean like carbonated beer in bottles?"

"No, banana beer. From the fermented juice of bananas. It is called *urwagwa*. It is actually a kind of wine, but everyone calls it 'beer.' Every Rwandan household knows how to make banana beer. It is a big part of the hospitality we share with one another. My father always made sure to have a jug of banana beer on hand to share with friends who would visit."

This was starting to get good. "What does it taste like?"

"Banana beer? You would probably think it was bitter and sour-tasting, like buttermilk, but I think it is delicious."

"Is it strong?"

"Hah! If you have more than one bowl, you'll fall over."

We spent the next two hours talking about banana beer—how to brew it, how to serve it, how it is shared among friends, and even enemies. He told me how the traditional system of local justice in Rwanda depended on this drink. After two warring men brought a grievance to a court of elders, they were supposed to reconcile with each other by sharing a gourd of that potent *urwagwa*. Paul's father had served on this council and had been a respected voice. This topic led us to an afternoon's worth of stories about the complicated ways Rwandans relate to one another, and to the important lessons that Paul had learned about friendship and forgiveness when he was a boy. The notion of alcohol being more of a tool than a drink helped, in some ways, to explain how he was able to be such a force for decency during the 1994 genocide—and how he was able to save lives by summoning the inner capacity to sit down and drink Scotch and make friendly chitchat with murderers while his own life hung in the balance. It was something not many of us would be able to do, but I think a part of his lifelong preparation for this task lay embedded within that proverb of his father's: "You never invite a man without a beer."

I had to silently thank my own father for his genial cussing all those years ago. It was the door to my learning about banana beer in Rwanda, and this detail of someone else's life. The road into another person's memories often begins with your own.

I'll tell one more story about Paul. After we had been working together for a while, I had the privilege of traveling to Rwanda to see the luxury hotel where Paul had sheltered the Tutsis during the genocide. I met many Rwandans. I drank banana beer (and yes, it has a flavor that I'll call "unique."). I also hired a car and driver and we bumped down miserably bad roads to get to the remote hill in the Ruvayaga Valley where Paul had been born and raised. Not far away from his father's house was the place where Paul went to school and learned to read—a private institution run by the Seventh-day Adventists' church. The modest, but handsome, campus had been built on a hilltop in 1921 by a couple of missionaries from Switzerland who had been sent to Africa to spread the gospel. They deliberately put the campus on the hilltop because it had been the site of many executions and was supposed to have been cursed by ghosts. The missionaries wanted to prove to the Rwandans that the missionaries' God was the only one. I walked around the grounds and looked at the classroom buildings, the soccer fields, the church painted blue that anchored the quadrangle.

The next time I visited Paul, we started to talk about his early education. Once again, he spoke only in general terms at first. He learned to read French at age eight and English at age thirteen. His exam scores had been poor during his first year, but he resolved to do better and wound up at the top of his class following year. Again, not bad stuff, and necessary information, but there was nothing there to make it unique—nothing that communicated the sweat and vigor and confusion that comes with even a boring childhood. There had to be a way into this, too, and we knocked around for about fifteen minutes before I thought again of the baby-blue church and imagined that it must have been filled with music at various times.

"Did your teachers teach you to memorize hymns?" I asked him.

"Oh, yes," he said. "That was part of our religious education."

"Did you have a favorite?"

He thought for a moment. Then he named a hymn and—to my astonishment—started to sing it for a few moments. It was a French song called "The Bookseller of Vaud," and it was about a tattered peddler from Switzerland who had only a Bible to sell to a beautiful lady of the aristocracy. She read it and her soul was saved. In translation, part of it goes:

> *Oh! Look at, my beautiful and noble lady,*
> *These gold chains, these invaluable jewels.*
> *You see these pearls of which the flame*
> *A flash of your eyes would erase?*

It is hard for me to explain, but Paul's childhood came to much fuller life for me when I heard him singing this song. More accurately, it was my being able to *see* him as a boy of ten, his voice drowned in a chorus of his friends, all dressed in uniforms of white shirts and blue shorts, singing this syrupy ditty about a white European woman inside a church in an obscure Rwandan outpost. There was an absurdity about it that seemed to evoke the entire colonial experience in Africa, and the twinned worlds that Paul had inhabited from his early childhood. He was the son of a rural banana farmer, true, but he was taught to sing songs about European aristocrats and gold chains many years before he ever saw either one in reality. It wasn't right and it wasn't wrong—it was just the way it had been for him.

I may be reading too much significance into this exchange, but all I can say is that at least I felt I understood more about Paul after I heard him sing those unlikely words in that low voice. Those lyrics went straight into the book we wrote together. It would not have been the same book without them. Such a little scrap of memory helped paint a picture of a whole life.

It was entirely natural for Paul not to have remembered that French hymn without a bit of prompting. All of us have a tendency to forget the minutia of life—the sour smell of a library book, the way the pockmarked man behind the coffee counter always calls us "chief," our habit of silently counting stair steps in our heads as we climb them. These are the beard-trimmings of ordinary existence, usually swept away from our minds as quickly as they fall, but they have boundless worlds of life inside. If you can arrange a few of them together in the right way, you can start to see the face behind the beard.

I'm telling you all this to highlight my belief that interviews can be a messy business. I've heard some journalists talk about the "art of the interview," but to my way of thinking, if interview is an art, it is certainly not a fine art. It's more like finger-painting. Ordinary conversations can be repetitive, scattered and rambling and so, too, can an interview. Even in its simplest state, an interview is nothing more than an exchange between two flawed and impatient people who are transferring some kind of understanding from one to the other. *"Senator, how many votes do you have lined up for this energy bill? Sixty-seven? Great, thanks!"*

But the best conversations—the ones we really remember best—go far beyond the mere transmission of fact. The best conversations lead us into a state of empathy for the other person. I have become convinced that this quality of empathy is one of the finest experiences available to us in our lives and one of the best possible states that can be passed between two people.

I heard the following statement once from the pulpit of a Presbyterian church and thought it was one of the wiser insights on relationships I'd encountered: "Nothing is sexier than really being known and understood."

The pastor happened to be referring to the mystery of marriage, but I think his insight extends beyond sexual love and into the general realm of friendship. The yearning to be read and appreciated by others is a universal hunger that also comes with a massive amount of fear. To be laid bare before another person is to risk judgment and rejection. Nevertheless, we still want very badly to be understood. All of us are condemned to live in a basic state of loneliness, our thoughts jailed in a shell of flesh and bone, inaccessible to anyone else except in the most rudimentary (and potentially deceptive) ways. Moments of true empathy are fleeting and rare.

These moments cannot be counterfeited and they are nothing you can learn or plan for. The path inward may be located unexpectedly in a long-forgotten curse word uttered in the kitchen. You often have to walk sideways, backwards, diagonally, and in circles with your subject before you can find the path that leads you to the banana beer or the French hymn. It may seem like a futile effort with a tight-lipped subject, but it *can* be done, and done by just about anyone.

I'm now going to talk more specifically about interview techniques and suggest several strategies for finding the good stuff inside your subject and doing justice to their impossibly rich lives—no matter who they are, or how little you feel you have in common with them at first.

DON'T ASK FOR A BORING RESPONSE

Q: *"What did you do for your first job?"*
A: *"I delivered newspapers when I was twelve."*
Q: *"Did you like it?*
A: *"Yeah."*

The better follow-up question is "Tell me what that was like," or better yet, "Tell me what an average morning was like for you." These kinds of open-ended queries will force your listener to come up with detailed remembrances on their own. That your grandfather enjoyed delivering the *Herald* doesn't make for very interesting reading, but his story of accidentally tossing the Sunday supplement through the Johnsons' plate-glass window sure does. Most of your questions should be aimed at gathering anecdotes.

DON'T ACCEPT A BORING RESPONSE

Q: *Tell me what an average morning was like for you.*
A: *Well, we folded the papers and then we delivered them.*

Q: *You threw them onto people's porches?*
A: *Yeah.*
Q: *And you were on a bicycle?*
A: *Yeah.*
Q: *That's pretty old-fashioned.*
A: *That was the way we did it back then.*
Q: *What job did you have after that?*

Yawn . . . There are so many more approaches this interviewer could have taken. How far could you throw a paper? What kind of practice did that require? How many times did you crash your bicycle? Did you always take the same route? What did you daydream about while on your bike? Did you use your bicycle to do wheelies or jump ditches? Who was the best delivery boy in town? How did your bosses pay/treat you? How did your parents feel about this job? And . . . need I say it? . . . ever break anything with a thrown paper? If something interests you, keep poking! Chances are excellent they'll eventually come out with an engaging story, or a fascinating piece of trivia.

One way to avoid boring answers is to refrain from asking a series of questions that lead inevitably to yes-or-no answers. With a quick turn of the wrench, you can turn a question from "closed-ended" to "open-ended" and get a marked difference in the quality of the replies. Notice the difference between these two questions:

- *Do you often take vacations?*
- *Where do you go on vacation?*

Both questions ask for essentially the same information. But see how the first one almost begs the listener to give a one-word answer? Phrasing the question with an open end is more likely to result in solid and original responses.

GET CONCRETE

Go fishing for vivid details—the kind of real-life ornamentation that brings color, dimension, and truth to a story. One of America's best regional newspapers, the *St. Petersburg* (Florida) *Times*, used to have a piece of advice for its beat reporters, a version of which is often repeated by the writing coach Roy Peter Clark. When covering a crime scene, the reporter should always get: "the name of the dog, the brand of the beer, the title of the TV show playing in the background." Those bits of real-life detail make it easy for the reader to picture that room as a familiar place. It puts the crime in sharper focus—makes it more *real*. Those checkered drapes and the Marilyn Monroe poster on the wall may seem irrelevant. They're not.

On-the-spot details bring a strange kind of glow to a story, one in which mysterious connections are made and invisible switches are thrown. "God is in the details," goes the old saying. History is incomplete without the details. Ordinary *life* is incomplete without the details. We didn't sit down tonight to eat "food," we sat down to eat a Porterhouse cooked rare, with mashed potatoes, a salad, and a Bombay martini with two olives. We didn't put on our socks in the morning, we put on thin black dress socks with little blue diamonds on them.

Here's another odd example of what I'm talking about. Over the years I've met several people who have a fascination with the Lizzie Borden hatchet murders of 1892 in Fall River, Massachusetts. Without fail, all of them can recite what was on the Bordens' table for breakfast that summer morning: mutton soup, sliced mutton, pancakes, bananas, pears, cookies, and coffee.

A disgusting spread, to be sure, and not really connected to the double homicide of Lizzie's parents that was soon to take place inside the house, but that breakfast is still an indispensable element. It speaks to the turgid and oppressive New England atmosphere inside the Borden home (you can almost taste that stale lamb on a hot morning) and holds a grim attraction more than a century later. That breakfast is an irresistible detail of the case.

I'll give you yet another example of the power of "irrelevant" detail. In the Bible, the twenty-fifth chapter of Genesis tells us of two brothers. Esau is the firstborn and a skilled hunter. Jacob is quiet and reserved, but secretly out to steal his brother's inheritance. So when Esau comes in from the fields one day tired and starving, Jacob won't let him have any food. "Quick, let me have some of that red stew!" demands Esau, but Jacob refuses to dish it out until Esau has given him the birthright of the first son in exchange for a single bowl. And so Esau squanders his entire inheritance for a bowl of red stew.

Red stew! It wasn't some vague "food." It wasn't an indeterminate "meal." The Bible is precise about this detail. It is a wonderful piece of data. And with the pathetic red stew in the middle of it, the story of Jacob and Esau somehow becomes a different story. A better story.

For yet another example, think of Albert Einstein. What do you see? Chances are excellent you see him at a blackboard chalking $E=mc^2$ and gazing at his listeners with that inimitable explosion of white hair. Einstein's significance to history is writing that formula; his hair is entirely irrelevant. Einstein's mane could have been slicked back, combed over, parted left, buzzed flat, shaved bald, dyed black, pick your style—and it wouldn't have made the slightest difference to his brilliance as a mathematician. But our conception of Einstein as a human being, even superficially, is diminished without the hair.

So when you're conducting your interview, ask questions that are designed to elicit details that may seem trivial, but nonetheless help set a mood and a view of what it was really like for the subject to be there. An excellent question is always: "Can you describe what he/she/it looked like?"

Almost no detail in our lives is truly irrelevant. What does this mean for you when you're listening to a description of your grandfather's home life during the 1950s? That's right: Get the name of the dog, the brand of the beer, the show that was playing on television.

Oh, and find out what his hair looked like.

NEVER TALK DOWN—OR UP

I hesitate to tell you this next story because I'm ashamed of it. But a single bad interaction I had with a stranger taught me more about interviewing than nearly anything I learned in any journalism class, so here you go.

One of my first jobs out of college was as a crime reporter in Savannah, Georgia. The city was at the tail end of a drug war and many of the murders that took place there were in a U-shaped belt of decaying Victorian houses surrounding the center of the city. One weekday afternoon, I went to this neighborhood to cover a stabbing. Somebody had been knifed while standing at a pay phone in front of a convenience store. There were loopy trails of blood on the sidewalk as if the victim had run back and forth after the stabbing. The police had quickly arrested a girlfriend, but weren't giving me anything else to go on, so I went knocking on the neighbors' doors in search of information. I came across an elderly man sitting on his porch and asked him if he knew anything about the girl. A little, he told me. What did I want to know?

Even today, years later, it makes me wince with embarrassment to say what my next question was: "So was he running around on her?"

I'm not sure where this stupid Erskine Caldwell dialogue came from, but I must have somehow thought it would help me establish a connection with this man. It was certainly not an expression I would have used with the cops, with my co-workers, with my friends, with my bosses, with just about anybody, for that matter, except an elderly Southern black man sitting on his porch in the sun. I will never forget his response. "Well, young man," he said, raising an index finger, "that is a question that requires deep thought and analysis and is one in which a conclusion may not be drawn too quickly." He then stared at me with silver eyes. What he was really saying, of course, was: "Get out of here, kid, you're patronizing me." And he was right.

I walked away feeling like a colossal jerk, and though I never even learned the man's name, he taught me this. *Never* adjust your mannerisms or speech to fit what you think another person might better understand. In fact, never pretend to be anybody other than the person you are. Be yourself, albeit a quiet and more curious version. You will get tons more respect this way. And authenticity is almost always given back in equal measure. The humorist P. J. O'Rourke once wrote: "People everywhere are exactly alike." He's right. And one of the things the entire world shares is an awareness of when the other person is trying to edit their basic personality.

So keep this commandment in mind: Thou Shalt Be Thyself.

DON'T ASK FOR A REFUSAL

There may be times in your interviews when you'll be treading on some sensitive ground. I'll have a lot more to say on the matter in Chapter 7, but for now, the thing to keep in mind is this: Avoid phrasing questions in such a way that it almost *invites* the subject to shut down when they might not want to.

I've certainly been guilty of this. In an attempt to make someone feel more comfortable about discussing embarrassing topics, I've gone out of my way to frame the question inside a kind of apology, and make sure to remind them that it's perfectly okay if we skip over certain things. But I don't think this kind of tiptoeing is helpful. Because when you say something like, "Would you be interested in talking about _____?" you're practically jumping up and down and waving a flag that says WARNING! in big red letters. You even plant the idea that talking about delicate subjects is socially unacceptable or would be a vague "bad idea." And because of an overdose of politeness, you miss out on an important conversation or revelation.

Leading questions aren't the only way to slam doors. Your body language, tone of voice, frequency of murmuring, or a hundred other little dots and dashes telegraphed across the room can unconsciously signal your belief that the other person *might* be uncomfortable with a certain topic. And this, ironically, will make them feel uncomfortable when they may otherwise have been at ease. You rob them of the chance to make their own decision.

So don't say, "Would it be okay to talk about your grandmother's suicide?" Instead, be honest about what you want to talk about. Relax your twitching pencil and nervous foot, and say in a forthright voice, "I'd like to hear about your grandmother's suicide." If they are uncomfortable, you'll be able to tell. And if they don't want to talk about it, you won't be pushy. You'll respect their wishes and move on. Simple as that. But wait for hard evidence before you make that judgment.

SILENCE IS YOUR FRIEND

Police detectives know this well: A great way to coax an untalkative person into saying something is to keep quiet yourself. If you create a little pocket of silence in the middle of a conversation, the other person will feel a powerful urge to fill it up with words. I don't know whether this comes from an innate sense of politeness or an unconscious aversion to awkwardness, but very few people can go more than fifteen seconds without breaking the silence.

The silence technique is most effective when you feel you've gotten a boring answer to a question, or a half answer. The last words hanging in the air will be the ones your subject will be most likely to latch onto for something to fill the air. Most likely, you'll get an elaboration. Silence can be enormously creative.

But it goes without saying that you should be judicious with this trick. You don't want to accidentally cast a sullen mood over the interview.

PIPE DOWN

A corollary to the above: You should also be careful in sharing your own opinions about whatever the subject is saying.
You may hear some disappointing things in the course of
these conversations, but you aren't likely to change the subject's mind with argument, nor will you be advancing the
primary cause of documenting a life if the discussion gets
contentious. Enthusiastic agreement is also dangerous if
the topic revolves around a sensitive family issue. Keep
your comments neutral and nonjudgmental.

This can get tricky, of course, if the subject asks you directly for an opinion. If you feel like that's a recipe for trouble,
try the diplomat's old trick of expressing vague sentiments in
the passive voice, such as "Well, I think it's always very sad
when fathers are let down by their children" or "We all say
things sometimes that we don't really mean because we're
confused and angry" or "It sounds like a lot of mistakes were
made in that situation."

THE MOST INTELLIGENT QUESTION IS . . .

"Why?"

RELAX

The best interviews feel like natural conversations with a
friend. Always aim for an easy conversational style. Also try
not to show any embarrassment or hesitation about the
endeavor—it can plant the subconscious idea in the subject's mind that this is somehow a threatening set of proceedings.

And although you're here to get good information,

avoid peppering your subject with rapid-fire questions. Let the stories emerge slowly, the way they do in more casual settings. We can sense when we're being interrogated, and few of us respond well to interrogation.

The journalist Owen Lattimore, who studied and wrote about Asia in the 1940s and 1950s, noticed something important about his interviews while traveling in Inner Mongolia. He wrote: "There is nothing that shuts off the speech of simple men like the suspicion that they are being pumped for information: while if they get over the feeling of strangeness they will yarn as they do among themselves. Then in their talk there comes out the rich rough ore of what they themselves accept as the truth about their lives and beliefs."

BE SENSITIVE TO MOODS

Not every day is going to be a talkative one for your subject, and you may have the bad fortune to catch them at a time when their thoughts don't flow easily or come laced with a dose of cantankerousness. Use your best judgment as to whether to declare it a "snow day" and just drink some wine or watch a movie with your subject, or whether to press forward in the hope of salvaging some useful conversation. If you do call it quits for the evening, do so with grace, but—important—don't let it become a habit. Resolve to pick up the conversation again next session.

DON'T LEAD THE WITNESS

Q: *So you delivered newspapers on a bicycle?*
A: *Yes. All the paperboys had about a hundred houses to cover. We had to get up at five A.M. to start folding the papers.*

Q: *Was it hard to rouse yourself out of bed at such an*
   early hour?
A: *Yes, I suppose.*

There are numerous ways that we can shape a subject's answers based on the words we use to frame the questions. Most of us do it inadvertently when we impress our own system of values onto the conversation. For example, don't ask, "How did it feel to be a solider in Vietnam when the country was so divided against the war?" Instead, be more open-ended in your phrasing and let the subject fill in the details and coloring that are most meaningful to them, such as, "How did it feel to be a solider in Vietnam during that period in American history?" People who take telephone polls have known this for years and the honest ones work hard to phrase their questions in neutral language. Make sure you're letting the subject express his own values instead of echoing yours.

BRING A TOOLKIT

Remember Brad Tyer from the previous chapter, who used a photo album to get his grandmother talking? This is an excellent way to stimulate good conversation if things start to drag. If possible, direct the subject's attention to some old photos, memorabilia, etc., to restart the conversation. Focusing on objects rather than people is a way to take some of the pressure off the exchange.

If you feel comfortable, you might consider asking the subject if they ever kept a diary or journal. And, of course, if they would mind sharing any of it. There is nothing like the original writings of a person to bring you inside their particular way of thinking—or of concealing.

GET IN THE CAR

One of my all-time favorite photos of Grandma was taken in a vacant lot at the corner of Polk Street and 14th Avenue in downtown Phoenix. There is nothing there now except a concrete slab, a desiccated palm tree, and a few weeds sticking up through the hardpan. This is the location of the simple frame house that her parents purchased in 1917 and where she grew up. There were chinaberry trees in the front yard and a drainage ditch that she used to jump over as a game.

The house was torn down many years ago and replaced by a block of apartments. Those, too, have been torn down; only the slab and the weeds and the palm are left.

We drove out together to the location one day in the spring of 2003, when she was eighty-eight years old, and I walked with her onto the vacant lot. She pointed out where the porch had stood, the approximate location of her bedroom, where her parents' had their own bedroom. I snapped my grandmother's photograph as she stood on this archeological site. And she talked about her father, Evan Arza Wilson, a veteran of the Spanish-American War who had worked as a door-to-door "laundry solicitor," going to people's houses with a horse-drawn cart, asking if they needed their clothes cleaned. He later hauled ice and worked as a constable.

While we talked, a fellow came down the street pushing a handcart. There was a bell on the handle. He was an ice cream man who did business with the children who now lived in the neighborhood. It was a hot day and I went over to see what he had in the cart. He opened the white lid for me.

"Mango popsicle?" he asked me.

"Sounds good," I said. "One mango popsicle."

Grandma and I shared it underneath the dying palm tree. Under our feet were shards of broken beer bottles and chips of tile from the vanished apartments. Except for the retreating bell of the ice cream man, it was quiet.

Driving your subject to important sites from their past can be an unforgettable experience. If it is possible, get in the car and take a trip back in time. You might be surprised at what you see.

LEARN FROM THE EXPERTS

Tune into David Letterman, Conan O'Brien, or Jay Leno for a few nights to watch how talk-show hosts guide a conversation. Many of the stories they extract from their celebrity guests are pre-arranged and somewhat canned, but their conversational styles should still be admired. Notice also how the host effortlessly steps out of the way of the guest to let them have the spotlight for a few minutes. Letterman, in particular, has a habit of drawing out guests by simply saying, "Now tell me about _____." It's a handy phrase to bring into your own interviews because it's more imperative than a question, it conveys the listener's genuine interest, and it also lacks the slight air of condescension that the phrase "Now tell *us* about _____" somehow carries. Oprah Winfrey is a genius at the craft of interview and I encourage you to observe how she does it smoothly and efficiently. If you don't watch television, try to find the afternoon radio program *Fresh Air* with Teri Gross on your local NPR station. Gross is consistently one of the best radio interviewers in the country.

HELPFUL MURMURS

Don't forget the courtesy of making occasional noises of encouragement while the person is in the midst of a discourse. Stony silence can make them afraid they're being boring and they may hustle to finish up just when it was starting to get good. Be prepared to salt in enough *hymmphs* and *wows* and *reallys* to season the air with approval and interest, but not so many that you make your interviewee think you're interrupting or wanting to get in a word yourself.

We all know what a good listener sounds like: unquiet enough to remind you they're still present, still engaged, still an active partner in the conversation, but sufficiently unobtrusive that we never feel as if they're waiting for us to finally get to the point and shut up so that *they* can start talking themselves.

A good way to maintain a presence without getting in the way is to use "nondirective" comments that remind the listener that you're on the same page. These are neutral statements. They do not express an opinion. *I see. Yes. I understand. Uh-huh. Wow. Okay.*

Think of these nondirective comments like dinging signals alongside the railroad tracks that you'd hear while on board a speeding train. They are there to mark passage, not to steer it.

BRIEF ENCOUNTERS

Don't lose interest if they start talking about an interaction that seems randomly chosen or out of context. In fact, perk up your ears. What a person chooses to share about a brief conversation or friendship can be revealing—not necessarily about themselves, but about the strange nature of life, and of memory. I still remember certain people who I once sat next to on a bus twenty years ago. I have no explanation for why, only that the bits of information that lodge in our minds must do so for a reason.

When my grandmother was talking about food one evening, she felt compelled to relate an odd recollection. This is from her biography:

During summers, [the family] went places in the Model A. There was a large apricot orchard in Scottsdale where they brought fruit by the case. Grapes were sold at an orchard at 48th and Thomas. They made jam and pies with the apricots and canned the grapes, which were "hideous" when canned, but good when fresh. They could snack on those, which was the only thing that was ever snacked upon. Except once: Ann was hungry down at her mother's place of work at the Maricopa County Recorder's Office. She begged for a nickel for a hamburger, and Mother, prodded by coworkers, relented. At a greasy spoon on Washington Street, Ann ordered before asking the price. It was ten cents. "But I have only a nickel," she said pathetically. "That's all right, I'll give you a nickel," said another customer.

"I don't think that man ever got a more grateful look in his life," Ann said. "I got my old greasy hamburger for a nickel."

We don't know that long-ago nickel-loaning stranger's name, or whatever happened to him. He is noted here only for this brief act of kindness. But you're reading about him today, a small memorial to that act.

END WELL

Close out each session on an upbeat note. Be sure to tell your subject how much you enjoyed the time and the stories. Make them feel good about having been open with you, and—if necessary—reassure them that they haven't bored you. Make it clear that you want to come back next week and do it again.

CASE STUDY

An Interview Observed

Three years before he died, Rebecca Skloot's grandfather, a man from southern Illinois, told his children and grandchildren that he had a confession to make.

"It's something I've wanted to talk about for a long time, but I couldn't," he said. "My brother Ronald and I were the only ones who admitted the truth; now he's dead, so I just have to tell you, even if it makes you mad."

After meandering around a bit more, he got to the point—his great-great-grandmother had been a woman named Elenor. And she had been black.

There was a long pause.

"Yes . . . *and?*" Rebecca remembers asking.

But for the family of her grandfather, whose name happened to be "Robert Lee," this was no small detail of genealogy. This was a major revelation. He had grown up in a different place and time: the lower Midwest of the 1920s and 1930s, where the Ku Klux Klan was a cultural force and the mores and prejudices of the post–Reconstruction South still carried great weight. Sexual relations between the races—known as miscegenation when children are produced—is one of the great taboo subjects of the old South, although it was hardly an uncommon practice from the moment that the first slaves were brought ashore. Perhaps the most emblematic case is that of Thomas Jefferson, author of the Declaration of Independence, who is believed by most historians to have carried on a long-running secret affair with one of his slaves, Sally Hemings, at his Virginia estate. A more recent icon, Senator Strom Thurmond of South Carolina, is known to have fathered an illegitimate daughter named Essie Mae Williams after an affair with his maid. He never publicly admitted the liaison, but never denied it, either, and he maintained a careful—though distant— friendship with Williams for the rest of his life. Old times are not forgotten in parts of the South, even in southern Illinois, and the consequences of being even "a little bit black" could have been socially devastating to a family eighty years ago.

But Robert Lee, known as Bob, felt it was time to come forward with what he knew and his granddaughter decided it was time to get him on tape. She conducted the following interview on August 18, 2001, when Bob was in poor health and breathing with the help of an oxygen tank. The conversation, punctuated with several coughing spells, is a remarkable exchange.

I'm including it here, edited slightly for clarity, because I want you to notice how Rebecca conducts herself—asking only simple questions to prompt Bob onward, and largely hanging back to let him tell the story at his own pace. Her unobtrusive style is demonstrated masterfully played out. Though the conversation rambles a bit, notice how she always manages to steer the focus back to a single subject.

Rebecca: *You know what I want to hear about? I want to hear about Elenor. I was so excited when my mom told the story you told her recently about one of the members of the family being a black woman. Where did she fit into all of this? And what was . . .*

Bob: Well, I didn't ever find out, fact is I was awfully dumb and naïve when I grew up because my, well, sometimes we'd go visiting somewhere in our surrey and horses and . . .

Rebecca: *On the horses?*

Bob: Horses pulling a surrey. And, say, if we came through Clay City on the way home, sometimes Mother would say, "Well, I think I ought to stop and see Uncle Newt." And they'd stop there and he was definitely a light-complected Negro. And he never married. And his last name was Blacklidge.

Rebecca: *Blacklidge?*

Bob: Yeah, Blacklidge. And my grandpa Lee's wife, who is my grandmother, was his sister, one of his sisters. And there were several of them, and their father, Mr. Blacklidge, he was a white man and this Blacklidge had several, he had several children. . . . Well, now, why I didn't ever start putting those all together, I don't know. It wasn't 'til Cynthia and I were married, and she was pregnant with [Rebecca's mother] Betsy, we lived over in southeastern Indiana, and we visited over in Grandpa Pettijohn's, one weekend in the fall, and those days, and it's pretty much the same now, in lots of cases, the folks after when we got the dishes washed and the kitchen kind of straightened up and they would come in the living room and sitting around and talk all afternoon and we'd be reminiscing and so on, and my aunt Mary and my aunt Bessie Pettijohn, my mother's two sisters, they were there . . . and I was half dozing, it was a sunny warm afternoon, we'd eaten a big dinner and essentially sitting there asleep, and I heard Aunt Mary say, "Well, they say her mother was black as the ace of spades," and I had kind of followed the train, and knew who they were talking about, and that really woke me up. . . . And so the mystery is, folks in the family that were working on genealogy, I mentioned this to them, and they said, "Well, that doesn't mean that we have black blood" [*said in mocking, exaggerated tone*] because there was another father and a step-relationship in there somewhere I could never get any explicit details on, but they don't like to talk about it, either, but another cousin of the Lees had a husband who had a job working with some business and I don't believe I ever knew exactly what the business was but he did a lot of traveling, and he had quite a little bit of free time and he got to study the Lee family and he told me, "Well, there's nothing very clear about it except that you go so far back with the Lees, you run into this black family, you know." [*Laughter*] That black family, their name was . . .

Rebecca: *Hickenbottom?*

Bob: Hickenbottom, yeah. And to me it sounds like a family that might have been slaves owned by the Hickenbottom family, that's a large name and it sounds to me like that's quite often where the names came from among blacks is they took the same name as their masters and so, and I know also over in Clay City cemetery where that fellow is buried, there is a Hickenbottom grave, it's off to the corner, it's a little brushy spot, couple or three trees, and under one of those oak trees there is a small stone, and they have a hand-chipped name of Hickenbottom. So you know that they're [*laughter*], I guess there are still Hickenbottoms live still in this area somewhere, and we're related to them.

Rebecca: *That must have struck something in you because you knew about this history and hadn't told anybody. Why hadn't you?*

Bob: Oh, yeah. Nobody would talk about it back then. But, well, the thing is that people shouldn't feel so concerned as they do, because most people—if you go back far enough—will run into relationships like that. We're all mixed if you go back.

Rebecca: *You know, I was excited, when my mom told me about this, I was very excited because I don't believe in separation of races—we're all the same, and I agree, if you go back far enough, you find this in a lot of families—I was really excited to know, the actual, the point when it happened, I think it's great.*

Bob: Well, my grandmother Lee, whose maiden name was Blacklidge, her mother was a Hickenbottom, and . . .

Rebecca: *So that makes Elenor your great-great-grandmother?*

Bob: Yeah.

Rebecca: *So what do you think the concern was? Why were people worried about this so much?*

Bob: I didn't hear you.

Rebecca: *[In a louder voice]: Why do you think people were so worried that they might have black blood?*

Bob: Well, I think it was part of the slave tradition. I was just reading last day or so, about [Thomas] Jefferson, you know, and his liaison with Sally Hemming, and there's always been a lot of argument over that, but he wouldn't admit it, but this I was reading, last night or night before, said that he's confirmed it, sooner or later.

Rebecca: *Like DNA testing?*

Bob: Yeah, yeah.

Rebecca: *And so do you think that people were worried that they would be associated with the slaves that people knew?*

Bob: Yeah, I guess. Boy, I had never talked to anybody in my family about it. . . . I didn't know who I could tell about it back then, who would react bad. But, no, I'm not concerned about it anymore, and I wouldn't be. I think it's nice to know.

4

Childhood and Adolescence

You're now ready to begin your walk through a life. Good questions will be your stepping-stones, and the path begins in childhood.

This portion of the interviews can be one of the best parts for both of you. For your subject, it's a chance to unlock pleasant memories of things and people they may not have remembered for years. For you, it's a chance to get a glimpse of a different world, and perhaps understand more about the building blocks of your subject's personality.

Before you start asking the questions, remember that even the toughest, strongest, most accomplished people who ever lived were once children who could not even feed themselves. We were all children and teenagers once and were given the freedom to act like nonadults. The passage of time evicted us from that country for good. But the ghost of the new still lives in the decaying body. So take a minute to picture your subject as a fragile infant, looking with utter incomprehension at a brand-new world. Forget their wrinkles, their graying hair, their bouts of crankiness and their grievances, and try to imagine them seventy years younger—tiny and pink and snuggled in the arms of their mother or father. Then imagine them a second time—as a gawky adolescent, complete with pimples and a hangdog facial expression.

This quick exercise has a way of humanizing people like nothing else. "From this perspective," says the philosopher Alain de Botton, "we are better able to express the sympathy and generosity that we all but naturally display toward the young, whom we tend to describe as naughty rather than bad, cheeky rather than arrogant."

I'm going to suggest some questions, listed below in no particular order, which have the power to jog some memories from the first eighteen years of a subject's life. Not every one of them is going to work in every situation. But if you keep throwing them out there, some are sure to trigger a good story. By no means should you feel the need to ask *all* of them; that would create a Homemade Biography the size of the *Encyclopedia Britanica*. Just sprinkle in a few of them if things start to drag.

You'll have to use your judgment on some of them; the subject might consider a few lines of inquiry silly or invasive. You might also strike an unexpected nerve—asking, for example, "Did you ever play with matches" to somebody whose carelessness with fire caused great damage or injury to a person years earlier. It's best not to try anyone's patience if you feel their irritation level rising, and you should also be sensitive if you feel a sense of discomfort over certain dicey questions. But probably most of these inquiries will be welcomed.

Bear in mind that a few of them have been phrased out of necessity in a "closed-ended" fashion, meaning that they have the potential to generate dull responses from particu larly laconic subjects. The best way around this, if you think there's something lurking there, is to immediately follow up with an open-ended question that forces the subject to give an answer that has to go beyond a mere "yes" or "no." (You: *Did you have a secret place where you hid things?* He: *No.* You: *Oh, okay. Well, where did you keep your spare money?*)

Remember: Always try to go beyond the question to dig for *concrete details*. If his best friend had a dog, get the name of the dog. If her father liked to drink Kool-Aid, get his favorite flavor. And if she had her first kiss in a movie theater, you'd better find out what movie was playing that night. If she claims not to remember, I think we can then assume it wasn't much of a kiss.

- What is your earliest memory?
- What was your nickname? Who gave it to you?
- What was your favorite nickname for a friend or acquaintance?
- Did anyone bestow a bad nickname on you?
- Were you ever cruel?
- What was the most thoughtful gift you received?
- What was the scariest ghost story you ever heard?
- What was your first pet? Were you ever disappointed in the pet?
- When was your earliest conception of death?
- Who was your worst childhood enemy?
- Do you remember the first time somebody sat you behind the wheel of a car?
- What is the worst-looking scar on your body? How did you get it?
- What was the best thing you ever tasted?
- What was the first song that really moved you?
- How often did you go to church?

- Were you afraid of sinning?
- Which of the relatives in your non-immediate family did you like the best?
- When you would play make-believe, where would you go? A magic kingdom? Outer space? A house in the suburbs?
- What was the closest moment you can recall with your brother/sister?
- Did you ever try to change your name?
- What would you have chosen for a new first name?
- When you experimented with your signature, what did you come up with?
- When you would doodle during boring classes, what would you draw?
- What did you think about your first teacher?
- Did you ever fall in love with a teacher?
- What was your favorite class?
- What was your favorite book as a child? As a twelve-year-old? As a seventeen-year-old?
- What was your favorite movie as a child? As a twelve-year-old? As a seventeen-year-old?
- Did you ever wish you could have traded lives with someone else? Who?
- Who was your hero?
- How did your conception of what you wanted to "do when you grew up" change and shift during your growing-up years?
- Did you make prank phone calls? What was your favorite ruse?
- Did you have a friendship with the mailman? The bus driver?
- Was there a particular piece of land—woods, wilderness, playground—that was "yours"?

- Was there a game or sport which you wanted to be good at, and then you *did* get good at it? We're you athletically frustrated in other areas?
- What talent did you wish to have?
- What was your greatest athletic triumph? Your greatest academic triumph?
- Who was your worst teacher?
- Who was your best?
- Did you ever get in trouble with the principal? With the police?
- What was the most humiliating thing you had to wear? Overalls? Bad shoes? Braces?
- What was your favorite item of clothing?
- Did you ever try to write poetry? A song? A play?
- How did you feel about the president? Were you political?
- Did you ever want to *be* president?
- Did you run for class office?
- When was your first kiss?
- When was your second kiss?
- Who was the great puppy love of your childhood?
- When did you first taste alcohol?
- What was the first time you traveled far from home?
- What is your best vacation memory?
- Did your parents worry about money? Do you think this influences your current views on money?
- Did your parents fight?
- How did they discipline you?
- Did you have a "potty mouth"?
- What was the first big city you saw?
- What kind of a diary did you keep?
- Did you ever try to dig a hole to China?
- Did you bite your nails? Suck your thumb?

- Did you have a fascination with another country? Another city?
- What did you do to tease your siblings? Were you teased by them?
- Did you ever have your heart broken?
- Who taught you to drive?
- What was your worst driving mistake?
- Did you sneak out without your parents knowing?
- Did you vandalize anything?
- Did you ever steal anything?
- Did you have a friend you eventually came to wish you'd never met?
- Did you have a boyfriend/girlfriend you wish you'd never met?
- How often did you go to parties? Dances?
- Where was your fantasy residence? In the mountains? Next to the ocean?
- Did you have a garden?
- Did you help with the cooking?
- When you looked at the stars, what did you think?
- Did you collect stamps? Pennies? Butterflies?
- What celebrity or person in the news did you admire? Did you hate?
- What was one of the kindest things a stranger did for you?
- What was a mean thing a stranger did?
- How often did you pray? What did you ask for?
- What kinds of games did you play at recess?
- What was the most boring book you read?
- What was your favorite lowbrow reading?
- What was your favorite card game? Go Fish? War? Poker?

- What household chore did you hate?
- What chore did you love?
- What smelled the best around the house?
- What smelled the worst to you?
- What did you do at your birthday parties?
- Did you get birthday presents?
- Did you ever play with matches?
- Where was your favorite hiding place in hide-and-seek?
- What trees did you climb?
- Did you ever try tennis or golf?
- Who was your sports idol?
- What school sports teams did you try out for?
- Did you ever want to be a musician?
- What hobbies did you have that irritated your parents?
- Did you catch bugs or frogs?
- Did you play with dolls? What was the doll's name?
- What was your favorite comic strip?
- Do you recall the time you first felt sexual feelings for someone?
- Who was the first person you saw of a different race?
- What was your initial conception of God?
- Were you frightened of God?
- Did you feel God was loving?
- Who were you most envious of?
- Who did you imitate? Why?
- How old were you when you first tasted coffee?
- Did you ever puff on a cigarette?
- What was your favorite color? To look at? To wear? Did your tastes change?
- What different time in history did you want to be born into?
- Did anybody read stories to you before you fell asleep?

- Were you afraid of monsters under the bed?
- What was your worst fear?
- Was there ever a fire in your house?
- Do you remember scary storms?
- Did your parents tell you about Santa Claus? The Easter Bunny?
- How did you find out the truth about Santa Claus and the Easter Bunny?
- Who told you about sex?
- What did you think of it?
- What did you think about death?
- Who was the first person close to you who died?
- What was the most amount of money you had as a child?
- Did you have a secret place to hide things?
- What was the worst scar on your skin you received during childhood?
- Did you think there was a man in the moon?
- Were you afraid of the dark?
- Who was the most popular girl/boy in your high school?
- Where did you want to go to college?
- Did you look at the clouds and make shapes out of them?
- Did you hear racially derogatory remarks, either about you or somebody else?
- What kind of volunteer work did you do?
- How did you feel about the army?
- What fashion of clothes did you really want to have?
- What fashion did you pick up that you now think was silly?
- What did you think "the future" was going to be like?
- Did you save old letters?

- At what points in your growing up did you feel like an outcast?
- What was the first real work of literature you tried to read?
- Did you ever carve your name onto anything?
- Did you ever wish to be a boy/girl?
- What was the time you were most courageous?
- What was the time when you were most cowardly?
- If you could go back and say one thing to somebody in your childhood, what would it be and who would you say it to?
- What was the first mountain you climbed?
- Was there a time you got lost, either in a town or in a wilderness?
- What did you like about animals? What did you not like?
- How old were you when you rode a bike for the first time?
- How old were you when you rode a horse for the first time?
- Did you ever laugh so hard that you peed your pants, or milk came out your nose?
- Did you have slumber parties?
- When was the first time you tried to stay up all night?
- Did you have nightmares?
- What offhanded remark, either positive or negative, has stuck with you?
- How were your grades?
- What was the most unfair grade you received, either in your favor or not?
- Did you want to be a grownup?
- Were you a good dancer?

- What was your favorite dance song?
- What was your standard approach to talking to the opposite sex?
- How did you try to get potential romantic partners to notice you?
- What was the strangest game you invented, either yourself alone or with friends?
- Besides being older and wiser, how have you changed the most since childhood/grade school/high school?
- Was your commute to and from school an adventure? How so?
- What smells do you most remember from childhood? What sounds?
- Did you ever run away from home?
- When was the first time you saw snow?
- When was the first time you saw the ocean?

CASE STUDY

Driving with Ms. Jody

Sharon Bond has deep roots in the city of Southern Pines, North Carolina. Her family on her mother's side had emigrated there from Scotland before the Revolutionary War. A proud and chivalrous ancestor of hers named Squire Shaw, a man prone to challenging his enemies to pistol duels on horseback, had built one of the oldest houses in town. The family still owned some fields of peach trees and tobacco a few miles outside the city limits. Sharon's parents had even met each other in a local bar, and so she could reasonably claim that she existed because of the town of Southern Pines.

But she still wanted to know more about what life had been like for the other members of her family, and so when a cousin's funeral brought her home, she took the opportunity to interview some of her relatives about their childhoods.

Because it seemed awkward to start a conversation simply by saying, "So . . . um . . . tell me about your childhood," Sharon hit upon the idea of getting in the car with her sixty-three-year-old aunt Jody and drive around to significant locations. They went first to a local cemetery and Sharon watched and took notes as her aunt pointed out the headstones of various ancestors and relatives. That seemed to prime the pump for stories and the rest of the day was spent visiting other places in and around Southern Pines that jogged Jody's memories of growing up there, picking tobacco in the fields, and sharing hard times with her sisters. Sharon took notes while Jody drove and talked.

"She hadn't been to some of these places for quite a while," said Sharon. "I think it really centered her. I could envision her playing like a little girl years ago at some of the places we visited that were important to her."

An auto or walking tour is a great way to get the conversation flowing if you happen to live in or be visiting the hometown of your subject. Significant geographical places in a person's childhood— a first house, an elementary school, a neighborhood playground— are like holy ground to most people. They carry a powerful psychic charge long into adulthood. And they can also be triggering points for some unexpected stories.

If you take a walking tour, be careful with the tape recorder— it may reproduce conversation garbled with car engine sounds or background noise, and be unusable. Better to take notes.

Also, be prepared for some free association that doesn't conform to a chronological account. Save the logical timeline for another visit. Traveling visits on foot or on wheels are likely to produce vivid but unorganized thoughts. Sharon compared it to "flipping through a stack of unorganized photographs."

It's usually better to remain silent than to talk during the interview process, but Sharon especially recommends quietness on your walk back through time.

"Let them set the pace for the conversation," she advises. "Let them unfold it as they will."

5

Adulthood

Near the end of his life, Mark Twain wrote in a letter to a friend: "I am old; I recognize it but I don't realize it. I wonder if a person ever really ceases to feel young."

I'm convinced that adults are often nothing more than children wearing bigger clothes. The act of growing old is an inevitable passage for most of us, but one which does not necessarily change our insecurities, likes and dislikes, basic beliefs about life, taste in friends, or capacity for happiness. Perhaps the complementary senses of *insecurity* and *possibility* that we knew when we were kids is the everyday oxygen of life. That intoxicating feeling we call "youth" may just be a permanent state. "In our innermost soul," observed the Hungarian psychoanalyst Sándor Ferenczi, "we are still children and we remain so throughout life."

The questions listed below will lead you into conversations that go deeper than the ones you'd have inside a coffee shop or at the neighborhood sports bar, but the atmosphere should be the same—respectful, curious, relaxed, and, above all, friendly.

Not all of the following questions are going to yield stellar answers. As always, feel free to pick and choose and even improvise on them. They are designed to be sparks for the campfire, not the fire itself.

- Who was your first real adult boyfriend/girlfriend?
- Who was the girl/boy to first break your heart?
- What do you think is the meaning of life?
- For whom did you cast your first vote for president?
- Which political figure have you admired the most?
- Which have you hated the most?
- What was the most regrettable episode of American history?
- What was the most honorable thing this country has done?
- What's the best part of growing older?
- What's the worst part?
- Which show or event on television or radio has affected you the most?
- What made you decide to have children when you did? Or what made you decide not to have children?
- What was the best vacation you ever had?
- Did you ever think about suicide?
- How have your feelings about God changed over the years?
- What magazines have you read over the years?
- Was there a time in your life that you think of as a real "turning point"?
- Did you ever have an interest in genealogy?
- What do you wish you could say now to your parents/ grandparents?

- Who were your best friends at various points in your adulthood?
- When was the first time you made love?
- When was the moment you knew you wanted to marry your spouse?
- Have you ever had someone close to you come out as gay?
- Have you had a gay friend who did not come out?
- What country have you never visited that you would like to go to?
- Of all the places/houses you've lived, which was your favorite?
- Have you ever bounced a check?
- Have you ever failed to make a rent/mortgage payment?
- Who would you consider the great unrequited love of your life?
- Was there ever a time when you thought you drank too much?
- What's the most illegal thing you've ever done?
- What dreams have you had that came true?
- When did you realize your children were truly grown-up and gone?
- What are some of the funniest things your children have said or done?
- How did you feel in the weeks after the birth of your first child?
- How did you tend to spend your evenings when you were a parent?
- What scared you the most about being a parent?
- What was your wedding ceremony like?
- What's the worst holiday you can recall?
- What is the thing you've accomplished, small or large, over which you've felt the most pride?

- How have your feelings about race changed over the years?
- Does a memorable conversation you once had with a stranger stick in your mind?
- What popular song has meant the most to you as an adult? Can you sing a few bars for me?
- Which religion, other than your own, sounds most appealing? Which one sounds the least appealing?
- How did you get along with your in-laws?
- Where did you like to grocery shop? Why?
- Which book did you read in college, or in general, that most influenced you?
- What frustrations have you had with church/worship?
- Have you had frustrations in *not* participating in church/not worshipping?
- What was the most complex relationship you ever had with a neighbor?
- Who is the most famous person you've ever crossed paths with?
- Have you ever left a bad tip or no tip in a restaurant?
- Have you ever given or received a piece of jewelry as a gift?
- What do you like to do on rainy days?
- How did you cope with stress on the job?
- Did you ever place wagers on sports events? With whom?
- Have you ever served on a jury?
- How many traffic tickets have you received in your life? Did you attempt to talk the cop out of giving you a ticket?
- What is your feeling about bars/nightclubs?
- What is your favorite alcoholic beverage? Nonalcoholic beverage?

- Were you afraid of not being able to provide for/play a good role in the family?
- What was the biggest cooking disaster you've had?
- What was the most chaotic holiday gathering?
- What was your most favorite regular walk?
- Which of the five senses are you the most glad for?
- What do you think about when you look at the stars?
- How would you describe your driving?
- Which newspapers did you read? Did you trust them?
- Has your name ever been in the newspaper?
- What was the best play or concert you've ever been to?
- Which character, either fictional or real, do you most admire?
- What was the hardest thing you've ever had to do in the way of self-sacrifice?
- Which political cause do you wish you had participated in, or which social cause do you wish you had "done more" for?
- Where were you when you found out about Pearl Harbor/the JFK assassination/the *Challenger* space shuttle explosion/9/11? What were your thoughts while it was happening?
- When was the last time you rode a bike?
- What did you think of your children's teachers?
- What did you think of your children's friends?
- Can you describe one of the romantic moments of your life?
- Are you afraid of dying?
- What would your obituary say about you? What would be the first line?
- How are your political views different now than when you were eighteen?

- Have you ever belonged to a union?
- Have you ever been fired or laid off?
- What is the hardest thing you ever had to witness with your own eyes?
- Have you ever walked out of a movie in disgust?
- Is there a commonly regarded vice that you think is overfeared?
- Which vice is truly the worst?
- What was the most misunderstood thing about the line of work that you pursued?
- What did you love most about your career?
- How were you idealistic in your job?
- How were you pragmatic?
- What musical recording have you played most often?
- Does being alone make you antsy or lonely?
- What scares you the most about the future of the country or planet?
- How many children would you have liked to have had?
- How did you feel when you passed the age of realistic childbearing years?
- How do you think you're similar to members of your generation?
- How do you think you're different?
- If you were to choose to have dinner with one person now living, who would it be?
- If you were to choose to have dinner with one historical figure, who would it be?
- Which event from world history would you travel back in time to change if you could?
- Which event from your own past would you change?
- How did you feel when gray started coming into your hair?

- Do you think there's a heaven?
- What was one of your indulgences at work—coffee, chocolate, glass of wine at lunch, etc.?
- Do you think old people can fall in love?
- How does love become different as you age?
- Which spectator sport has been most consistently entertaining to you over the years? Why?
- Which popular sport has no interest for you?
- Why is the music of your youth the best music of all time?
- Do you like staying in hotel rooms? Why or why not?
- If you were going to start a small business, or start another one, what would it be?
- Had anyone you known been murdered?
- Whose role model have you been?
- What did you think your retirement would be like?
- What do you consider your most unwise purchase?
- What's the best use of a big splurge you experienced?
- What did you love most about your spouse?
- Which is your least favorite household chore?
- Are you lucky in cards, board games, etc.? Do you believe in luck?
- Which feature of yours is most attractive?
- What strikes you as one of the most unfair aspects of life?
- What kind of dish can you cook that nobody else can? What's the recipe?
- Have you ever been afraid for your personal safety because of war or terrorism?
- What is the finest city you've ever seen?
- Do you think people can really change or redeem themselves?

- Now that you're an adult, how is your relationship different with your siblings?
- Do you ever cry in movies? Which ones?
- Which physical changes have come to your hometown that most stand out?
- Did you ever feel like quitting a job? Did you actually do it?
- What has been the most welcome technological change since you were a child?
- Did you get along with your neighbors? Why or why not?
- What has been the most destructive advance in technology in your lifetime?
- What would you like to be remembered for?
- How ill have you ever become, and what was the cause?
- If you were made Monarch of the World, what's the first change you would order?
- What were some of the best holiday traditions you brought to your own family as an adult?
- What was the best "inside joke" you had as a family?
- What was your honeymoon like?
- Which are the five most influential books you've ever read?

CASE STUDY

Conversations About Adulthood

Ray Ring Jr. knew that the memories of his elderly mother were beginning to fade away with age, and so he resolved to preserve what he could. But he never quite bargained on the revelations that poured forth from eighty-four-year-old Kathryn Moore Ring when he visited her at her retirement home bearing a tape recorder.

It turned out that Ray's grandfather had been a pilot who had a rakish courtship with a woman he met near an air force base in Oklahoma. The accidental result of that union had been Ray's mother, Kathryn. She never got a chance to know her biological father. The daredevil pilot died in 1935 when his plane crashed in a Montana canyon—not far from the town where Ray now lives.

But this was only the beginning of an extraordinary story. Ray learned that his own dad, Ray Sr., had first been romantically entangled not with his mother but with his *grandmother*—the same one who had romanced the pilot during the Depression. It was reminiscent of *The Graduate*. The grandmother had always resented her daughter after Ray Sr. took up with her, and never again referred to her former boyfriend (now, awkwardly enough, her son-in-law) by his first name, calling him only "Ring." She later went on to become the chief counsel of a major soft drink corporation, burning through many other men along the way.

These were events buried in the past of which Ray had been only dimly aware until he showed up with the tape recorder. But they helped shed light on patterns in his family and in his life. Far from being uneasy about some of the uncomfortable facts of her life, Kathryn seemed eager to talk, and grateful that her son was asking.

"I never once got a sense that I was pushing her too hard," he said. The only limitation seemed to be Kathryn's level of energy. She would grow tired after a few hours of talking and Ray would always end the day's session when he felt she was drooping.

"Repeated interviews are good," Ray advises, "both for expanding the interview to additional periods of the person's life, and for going over the same periods again and again, because new memories keep coming up."

Keeping all the information straight was a challenge, but Ray managed it by holding to a chronological line. He didn't jump around from point to point in Kathryn's life, but used her birth as a starting point and moved it forward from there. "And then what happened?" was his constant question. In this way, he got a view of her life structured in linear time, with a few odd flashbacks here and there, as in a novel.

Ray has since visited the Montana canyon where the plane bearing his grandfather crashed in 1935. A copy of the front page of Butte's *Montana Standard,* which reported the accident, is now in his files. And Ray has made contact with some of his previously unknown cousins, offspring of more children that the pilot had fathered in Seattle before he died.

Listening to Kathryn talk about her life in such detail was one of the best memories he has of her, and of their relationship.

"There's a human instinct to tell a story," said Ray. "And we honor people when we ask them to tell theirs. It is an act of respect. And these stories often open doors that we don't expect. This project helped me understand myself more. I've become more accepting of my own failures, the places where I could do better, and seen why I've had a family life that's been very different from the one I grew up with."

6

Looking for Themes

Stories will never go away. They are the containers in which we store our memories and the tools we use to explain the absurdities of life to ourselves and to others.

Deep inside a person, just as in a movie or a piece of music, we can see patterns flowing and themes coalescing. The need for a father-figure, the frustrating search for acceptance, the constant risk taking, the love-killing perfectionism: these may be but some of the forces that frighten us, motivate us, inspire us, or follow us throughout our wanderings. These returning patterns are the "throughlines"—the binding threads of consistency and purpose that hold a life-narrative together.

They are not necessarily easy to find, or to explain with any clarity. The German poet Rainer Maria Rilke set this very hard standard: "All of us have been born with a letter inside us, and only if we are true to ourselves will we be allowed to read the letter before we die." This chapter won't necessarily tell you how to find that letter buried inside your subject; I believe this kind of work must be a solitary activity. But it may well give you clues that point in the right direction, and tell you how to recognize and highlight the general motivating factors in your subject's walk through this life.

Everybody has those motivating factors. In the opening lines of his remarkable book about careers, *What Should I Do with My Life?* the author Po Bronson says: "We are all writing the story of our life. We want to know what it's 'about,' what are its themes and which theme is on the rise. We demand of it something deeper, or richer, or more substantive."

These moments of self-inventory are universal, even among the least introspective people. At some point in the past, your subject has almost certainly asked themselves tough questions: Where am I going? What is this all for? What does my life really mean? These are considerations which could not only make for some of the most revealing conversations you'll have with your subject, but might also provide fodder for pivotal sections in the manuscript you eventually write.

It may well be that you decide not to weave a theme into your written biography, and that can be a perfectly honorable choice. As you'll see, searching for a theme can be an elusive—and even potentially divisive—exercise that should be undertaken after a good deal of thought and compassion. But even if you choose not to pursue a theme, I encourage you to at least look for one during the interview sessions. Stories are not just the vessels by which we teach ourselves, they are also the mini movies through which we pass along wisdom to others. Theme teaches us and links us.

In many ways, theme *is* us.

INTERVIEWING FOR THEME

The key questions to ask

The American journalist John Gunther reported from most of the nations on the globe in the course of his long career. He was a reporter for the now-defunct *Chicago Daily News*, but he is perhaps best known for writing the hugely successful "Inside" series of books, including *Inside U.S.A.* and *Inside Europe*. Whenever Gunther visited a new place, which was often, he always liked to ask two questions of the locals: (1) What makes this place distinct? (2) Who runs this place? These questions worked because they were irresistible to the recipients. The first appeals to a sense of regional pride, the second to the human love of gossip and intrigue.

You can ask a variation of these questions in your attempt to understand your subject better. As you near the end of your interview series, consider asking the following two questions, phrased in your own words:

- What has made your life distinct?
- What has governed your major decisions?

These are awfully probing questions, of course, and if you ask them cold, the response you'll receive is likely to sound a lot like "Huh?" Be sure to ask them only after you've established a trusting rapport, and only after you've heard a good many of your subject's stories. The questions might be tailored to fit specific episodes, such as: "When you told me about your decision to leave the navy and go to law school, it reminded me of how you also didn't want to go into business with your father back in Ohio. Is it accurate to say that looking for new challenges has always been a part of what drives you? Or does it stem from skepticism about authority?"

Gunther himself had this to say about his journalistic mission: "What interested me was not news, but appraisal. What I sought was to grasp the flavor of a man, his texture, his impact, what he stood for, what he believed in, what made him what he was and what color he gave to the fabric of his time." That's an admirable philosophy of reportage, and a perfect crystallization of what a Homemade Biography is about.

A related inquiry

A newspaper colleague of mine told me that whenever she was interviewing someone who didn't seem all that exciting, she would silently ask herself two questions: "How is this person like others of his mold?" and "How is he different?" I think this is an excellent method for trying to isolate that quality of uniqueness that lies inside each person. When interviewing the county tax commissioner, for example, my colleague might have wondered: *What is it about issuing home property assessments that he sees differently than other bureaucrats? What does he agree with? What does he disagree with? Does he think there's something immoral about using people's houses to build up a government's wealth? Or does he think we don't go far enough?* Asking herself these speculative questions helped her formulate the questions she actually posed to her subjects during the interview (and probably saved her from boredom during some otherwise deadly conversations). I'm not saying that asking yourself these questions is necessarily going to yield earthshaking insights on your subject, or reveal information that's going to change your life, but doing so can help brush a little color onto a gray shell.

What have they been chasing?

The British novelist and critic C. S. Lewis used the simple idea of "joy" as the connecting fiber in his autobiography. He had come to realize that this elusive feeling was at the heart of his life's pursuit, and had led him from a childhood fascination with Old Norse myths to adult interests in Greek poetry and theism and, finally, to a conversion to Christianity. The quest for the sublime fire that had dwelt inside since his childhood—he called it *North*—was a signpost to larger truths for Lewis, and therefore played a starring role in his memoirs.

A darker portrayal of "questing" was expressed in Thomas Hardy's novel *Return of the Native*. The beautiful Eustacia Vye cannot stop pining after an imagined cosmopolitan life in Paris, far away from her home in the English countryside. This lust for urbanity becomes a prime factor in her life, leading her to start a disastrous affair and cause her death.

While your subject's life may lack the melodrama of these two examples, it is likely that a constant desire for something—education, adventure, sex, a loving family, financial security, a better community, God, duty, avoidance of commitment—has fueled their choices at various points, or even all their life. If you see the same motivators popping up here and there in your subject's life, train your questions upon them and see what happens.

Don't accept a boring assessment

Many people, my grandmother included, grew up in cultures and families in which bragging or complaining was taboo and modesty was prized. When asked to assess their lives, they may adopt a stoical attitude and wave you off with a self-deprecating dismissal: "I've led a pretty dull life" or "I can't see that anybody would be interested in all these old stories." Don't believe it for a minute. They have seen things that nobody else ever will, and they have a lot of wisdom to share, if only by example. Ralph Waldo Emerson tried to remember a simple rule in all his conversations: "Every man I meet is in some way my superior, and in that, I can learn from him." It is especially important to keep this truism in mind when you're talking with an older person, who has seen and struggled with much more that can be easily discussed. The psychiatrist and philosopher Viktor Frankl wrote that senior citizens carry with them the "invisible granaries" of their accumulated life experiences. Tapping those granaries takes patience.

Your subject has much to teach the descendants she will never meet, even if she disagrees. A good strategy here is to speak encouragingly, and from the heart. Say something like, "I know it may not seem like it, but I think you've lived through interesting times and been through things that are remarkable to me." They may still come back with something flat like, "Well, I guess the story of my life is making the best I could out of my circumstances," but it's still a good starting point to elicit something more distinctive.

Hunt around

When reading over the manuscript for grammar and spelling, also be on the watch for recurring patterns. Don't be afraid to initiate another conversation to explore or expand on the chords you may have failed to hear the first time around.

Maintain an open mind

In general, don't start a biography with a theme already decided, no matter how well you think you know the person. You may have made a credible choice of "arrows" with which to guide you through another life, but you risk closing off other dimensions of the person that might surprise you. Ideally, the theme should creep up on you.

The dangers of armchair psychoanalysis

This is going to sound counter to what I've just been preaching, but it does pay to exercise a degree of caution when attempting to express themes in a subject's life. Your hunt for a defining aspect is undertaken in an innocent spirit, but people are complicated and can be sensitive about being casually weighed and boxed (and who can blame them?). Few of us will reach the end of our lives with anything resembling a total understanding of what turns our innermost gears, and this almost certainly includes your subject. So you should therefore avoid exerting too much certainty about things which are rich and unique, particularly the jewels of a life not your own. It is an excellent idea to approach these conversations with humility and a willingness to be told you are wrong—even if you believe otherwise.

WRITING FOR THEME

Phrase it briefly to yourself

Whenever I had a long and complicated newspaper story to write, I would sometimes ask the following question to get my thoughts in order: *What is the essential element of this story, in just one sentence?* I would then type the sentence at the top of the document as a kind of "fountainhead" for every other word that would follow. Any one of the following fragments could serve as a fountainhead phrase for your subject's biography:

- The search for love
- Triumph over addiction
- Love of country
- Disappointment with career
- Fear of poverty
- Search for religious faith (either successful or unsuccessful)
- Restlessness
- More acted upon than acting
- Always thinking of others

Playing it *pianissimo*

You don't necessarily need to spell out your theme explicitly as you write the life story. But you can use it as a guideline to arrange the material. Writers sometimes talk about the "arrows" that run sightlessly through their material, puncturing each paragraph with invisible holes and pulling the whole ball of words together with an invisible thread. One example of this in a Homemade Biography might be a subject whose life has been defined by their devotion to God or a particular church. You would have discovered during the interview phase that all the milestones of their life tend to be viewed in a religious light, and those reflections would certainly be an appropriate part of the material. Or, if the subject had always been disappointed with work or with family, these feelings, too, would come out naturally in the description of individual incidents.

Playing it *fortissimo*

If you've thought it over and had an honest conversation with your subject about a theme you perceive in their life, then you should feel free to foreground that theme, as follows: *Mildred Kershaw spent fifty years of her life looking for someone to see her as she wanted to be seen. She finally found it in her husband, Bert. This is the story of a very long search for love.*

The rest of the biography would be a standard retelling of a life story, except that most of the incidents and facts you'd relate in the manuscript—a father who was never home, being snubbed in high school, feeling isolated at her first job, and so on—would be working toward the "conclusion" of the theme: achieving confidence, and marrying Bert.

Over the horizon

The most succinct piece of advice on writing ever dispensed, comes from the British novelist E. M. Forster, who said: "Only connect." Be aware that the big themes represented in any one event are almost guaranteed to spill over the edges. They will show up elsewhere, through the stories that he or she chooses to share. So pay close attention to anecdote selection—it will tell you a great deal.

Let's say you've been talking to your subject about getting fired from a job mowing lawns while in high school. It's obvious that this somewhat minor event still bothers him after fifty years. What may be going on can be summed up in one word: *failure*. For him, it was likely not just a failure to show up on time to cut the Knickmeyer's grass. It spoke to larger post-adolescent fears of not being good enough.

I'm not saying that failure, or even the fear of failure, needs to be the all-encompassing Rosebud of this hypothetical biography. But it is enough to be aware that major life themes often lurk behind the individual events that your subject has decided to share.

Pivotal events

I've always felt sorry for private citizens who became famous for an unwitting act. Remember Steve Bartman, the Chicago benefits consultant and Cubs fan who accidentally knocked a fly ball out of the hands of outfielder Moisés Alou and was widely blamed for ruining the Cubs' 2003 season? Or how about Richard Jewel, the security guard who found an explosive that was about to go off at the 1996 Atlanta Olympic Games, and subsequently found himself besteged by police and reporters who believed him to be the bomber? Perhaps the quintessential example of unwanted American fame is that of Dr. Samuel Mudd, who bandaged the broken leg of a patient who turned out to be fugitive John Wilkes Booth, Lincoln's assassin? For whatever else they may have done or accomplished or worked for, however kind or decent they are as people, no matter how good a parent or child or employee they may happen to be, it will be that one random act—occupying a particular space at a particular time—that becomes their defining moment, and it will stick with them as long as they draw air. It will be the opening line in their obituaries. When people will talk of being related to them, or having been friends with them, it will be prefaced with "You remember that guy who . . . ?"

Few of us will ever be at the center of a media squall (and thank God for that) but there are moments in everyone's life in which trivial actions turn out to have major consequences. A missed train that leads to the first encounter with a new friend or love interest. The crash of an automobile or plane that steals a loved one, or creates a debilitating injury. The unexpected phone call from a half-remembered business acquaintance that leads to a new job and a change of city. Ronald Reagan wrote about his desire to transfer from tiny Eureka College in Illinois and having changed his mind at the last minute because it was raining on the day he went to visit the University of Wisconsin. It is conceivable his life's path would have been very different had it not been raining that spring day in 1929: He may well have settled into a business career in the Midwest and never made it to Hollywood, and then to the White House.

You lack the eyes of God and cannot see the total wave effect that small events may have had on your subject's journey through life, but a few moments can be clearly identified as turning points. If one really stands out, it might be worth building the narrative around it as the "lead anecdote"—the story that begins the biography. Example: *Although Sarah Hopkins could not have realized it at the time, her decision to spend Thanksgiving of 1964 serving meals in a homeless shelter may have been the most important meal of her life. It was where she realized that she felt a powerful urge to help those in need. This was the beginning of, as she said later, "my career as a social worker."*

Don't fear the contradictions

Nobody is going to benefit if you write a sycophantic and airbrushed portrait of your subject that ignores the real sweat and uncertainty of life. Worst of all, you'll bore the socks off whoever stumbles across this manuscript in a trunk two hundred years from now. They won't want to read timid clichés about their great-great-great-great-grandmother. They'll want to know the truth of what the lady was really like.

Seek the universal

This might also be phrased "Let the universal seek *you*," because major themes likely to emerge from a Homemade Biography are guaranteed to connect with larger patterns in the human experience. You will more than likely feel what novelist and whale-watcher Herman Melville called "the shock of recognition" in seeing shades and figures from your own life in the currents of another's. We are under sentence in this world to live inside our own minds, a lonely place, but there are those invisible fibers of shared experience and common feeling (disappointment, insecurity, elation, shame, bravado) that we can recognize in one another. This is what creates that quality of empathy between people that makes love possible and life bearable. The Roman playwright Terence famously said: "I am a man, and I hold that nothing human is alien to me."

More recently, Samuel G. Freedman, a columnist for *The New York Times*, has talked about what he calls the "Periodic Table of Human Nature," which he says is similar to the well-known Periodic Table of the Elements in chemistry. Just as every intricate object in the world can be ultimately reduced to a collection of molecular elements—carbon, silicon, hydrogen, phosphorous—so too can complex personalities be made understandable through their mixture of simple and universal human traits—greed, envy, joy, guilt, sacrifice. None of those feelings will be things you haven't experienced firsthand. And so you can hear and recognize familiar notes within the strange.

This aspect of the project may surprise you with its grandeur. There is almost no pattern within your subject's story that is beyond your comprehension, or even sympathy.

CASE STUDY

Message in a Bottle

When Kristin Gilger set out in 1998 to write the history of her family, there was no doubt in her mind what the organizing principle would be.

At the time, Kristin was the managing editor of the Salem (Oregon) *Statesman Journal*, which was embarking on a major project exploring the effects of alcoholism on Oregon's capital city. Kristin's own family had been affected by drinking for generations. And so Kristin told the readers of the *Statesman Journal* the account of her family, as viewed through the bottom of a glass.

The story began with these simple, powerful sentences: "I am what I am because of alcohol. It shaped me. It shaped every one of my seven brothers and sisters. It made us strong and it made us hurt at the same time. It still does. My history, tangled up as it is with drinking, is no different from the histories of millions of other families who cannot recall a family gathering, retell a family story or look through a photo album without a twinge of regret."

The presence of alcohol was far from the only thing happening in the life of the Gradys, a large working-class Catholic family in 1950s Cedar Rapids, Iowa. But it was the factor that always seemed to cause the most unhappiness, the thing that left its mark on every kid in the family. Kristin will never forget having her first baby and seeing her mother arrive too drunk to help out. Her sister Patty remembers that their mom and dad didn't come to her high school graduation because they were too far in the bag. Another sister was always falling into relationships with men she felt sorry for, a pattern she had picked up from her alcoholic parents. The unifying theme in the family's history was obvious, and not just because the newspaper Kristin worked for happened to be doing a project on the subject.

Kristin is an old newsroom boss of mine, and one for whom I have great respect, so I went to speak with her in her office at Arizona State University about the tricky business of searching for themes in people's lives.

She told me that the alcoholism was not only an obvious connector in the relationships within her family, it also provided a window to tell a larger story about a midwestern family in a state of confusion and denial.

"If I had set out to write about my mother's life just on its own, I wouldn't have known where to begin," Kristin told me. "This [alcoholism] gave me an arrow. It informed all my questions."

Depressing and painful as it was, this theme was inevitable if anybody wanted to tell the real story of the Grady family.

"Alcohol touched on everything in our lives," said Kristin. "If I had said to Mom, 'So . . . tell me about growing up,' alcohol inevitably would have come up. It overshadowed everything."

Kristin wound up interviewing four members of her family and came away with several hours of tape recordings which she turned into remarkable first-person narratives from each family member's point of view. Her sixty-eight-year-old mother, for instance, observed: "And then it got to the point where you couldn't have any fun without drinking. It was impossible. For years, I could drink anybody under the table. That changed. Your body won't tolerate it anymore. Then you start losing your tolerance, and when you used to have fun drinking, the drinking itself becomes the point, and you don't have fun anymore."

The series, which included stories from other *Statesman Journal* reporters, went on to win several journalism awards. It was not an easy exercise for Kristin. But it was ultimately a rewarding one for her personally. Strangers came up to her in the grocery store and shared their own painful struggles with alcohol. It brought her a keener understanding of her parents' struggles and a more compassionate view of the mistakes that had been made in her upbringing.

Theme limits a project, but theme also broadens a project. Sticking to alcohol as her "arrow," for example, made her realize that booze was hardly the only demon in the family and that the excessive drinking stemmed, in part, from other torments. It turned out that her father, John, lost his own father in an accident on the Rock Island Railroad. His mother got remarried to a store owner who was also a thief and an abuser who made John miserable. He couldn't wait to get away from home and volunteered for service in World War II just to get out of Iowa. Whatever he had seen in combat must have been horrific because when he returned, he got a bottle of Jim Beam, took his army uniforms out to the backyard, and set them on fire. He swigged the whiskey and watched them burn. John could talk about this only after he turned eighty and time had started to mellow him. And it occurred to Kristin only after she had completed the project that her father had had such a hard time being a father because he never had a father himself.

Her mother's road was difficult in its own way. She was forced to pass up a scholarship to the University of Iowa and fell into marriage because she believed it was expected of her. She always felt ambivalent about being a wife and a mother of eight children, but in her mind, her Catholic upbringing demanded she play this role. Drinking was her escape valve. But her story might just as easily have had the "arrow" of what it was like to be a woman of her time—or of any time—who sacrifices her desires for the sake of a larger purpose.

I asked Kristin whether she had any advice for those who also sought to document their family histories through the lens of a troubling subject. Because she is a journalist who is concerned about morality and ethics above almost all else, I was not surprised by her answer: "You have to be honest, and honesty can hurt people. If you can't be honest, don't write it."

7

Minefields

A s you've probably guessed by now, this project can be
as dangerous as nitroglycerin if used improperly. A
Homemade Biography has the potential to set off real family conflict. It can trigger stories you'd rather not hear. It
can also unearth searing resentments, expose dirty laundry,
or bring to light some long-repressed unpleasantness that
might have been better off left submerged. Subjects can become embarrassed and offended. Readers can be wounded
by harsh characterizations. If you're not careful, it can create an explosion.

Bear in mind, however, that nitroglycerin doesn't just
blow things up. It's also used as an effective heart medica-
tion. Just as any powerful tool can be used in the service of
good as well as of destruction, a Homemade Biography can
heal old wounds, make seniors recall the good times, ease
some of the loneliness and isolation that inevitably comes
with growing old, and bring people from different generations closer together. Most of all, it has the power to open

up new vistas of compassion and understanding between people who might not have ever discussed anything more important than the flowers in the yard or what's for dinner.

So you should not go into this endeavor overly afraid of what you might dig up, or intimidated by the perceived judgment of others. You must only be sensitive in how you handle the information and deal with the feelings of your subject. This chapter is a guide to some of the most common land mines that Homemade Biography can inadvertently set off, and the ways you can defuse them ahead of time.

TALKING TO PEOPLE WITH ALZHEIMER'S DISEASE

I sincerely hope you won't be confronted with this. Alzheimer's is one of the cruelest ways to lose anyone close to you because the disease relentlessly eats away not just a person's body. It consumes their personality, their irreplaceable store of memories, and everything else that makes them who they are. The mind becomes permanently choked with snow; once vibrant and funny people can only moan and stare. William Shakespeare probably had Alzheimer's in mind when he wrote the famous "acts of man" speech in *As You Like It*: "Last scene of all that ends this strange eventful history, is second childishness and mere oblivion, sans teeth, sans eyes, sans teeth, sans everything."

Previously classified as "senility," and regarded as a natural byproduct of getting old, we now know that Alzheimer's is anything but natural. It is a serious physical disorder on the level of muscular dystrophy or chronic diabetes, and up to ten percent of those lucky enough to live past age sixty-five will develop it. About two percent of America has it right now.

It is still possible to attempt a partial Homemade Biography with people in the early stages of Alzheimer's. And it is, of course, vital to not delay for another minute this act of preservation, because their memories will be suffocated in plaque all too quickly.

Before we talk about how you can get the most out of this experience, it's necessary to understand a little bit of the physiology and stages of the disease.

Alzheimer's was first identified as a specific disease of the brain in 1907 by a German psychiatrist named Alois Alzheimer. It begins with a cement-like protein called amyloid beta which begins to accumulate outside the nerve cells of the brain. At the same time, protein may be forming inside the nerve cells, as a weed grows around a pillar. Eventually, the amyloid outside the cells forms into clumps known as plaque, and the amyloid inside the cells grows into twisted strands known as tangles. These blockages impede the normal activity of the mind and cells begin to die. The effect over time is quite pronounced—the brains of Alzheimer's patients literally shrink in size and grow yellowish and discolored. The effect is not unlike that of the lungs of heavy smokers. Unless the victim dies of other diseases, the effect is always fatal because the plaque and tangles eventually reach the motor control center at the core of the brain and prevent the person from swallowing and breathing.

There is not yet a clinical test for Alzheimer's disease. The diagnosis is most always an educated guess from a physician who observes behavior and symptoms and asks a series of questions. The diagnosis usually turns out to be correct, but only an autopsy can reveal the presence of the telltale plaque in the brain.

This disorder should not be confused with the occasional slips in recall that come with growing older. Alzheimer's represents a progressive and systematic loss of normal functioning. The classic early symptoms go beyond forgetting a memorized line of poetry or misplacing the car keys. They include:

- Difficulty performing familiar tasks, such as forgetting how to make a sandwich
- Problems with basic language, such as saying "that thing that lights up" instead of "lamp"
- Mood swings, crying for no reason, or sudden bursts of irrational rage
- Radical personality changes
- Getting lost in one's own home or neighborhood
- Loss of motivation, such as sitting still in a room for hours
- Poor judgment, such as spending money foolishly or dressing for the beach on a cold winter day
- Grossly misplacing things, such as putting a book in the refrigerator.

Physicians at New York University have identified seven stages of Alzheimer's disease. Your ability to extract a quality biography will depend greatly on where your subject falls on this scale:

1. **No impairment** Proteins have begun to form, but the patient's memory is still sharp.
2. **Very mild cognitive decline** There are lapses in memory or slight personality shifts that may not be apparent to loved ones or to a doctor during a clinical visit.

3. **Mild cognitive decline** Language problems become noticeable to friends and family. There will be difficulty forming "new memories." Passages just read from a book or new people's names are quickly forgotten.

4. **Moderate cognitive decline** The ability to perform complex tasks, such as preparing dinner or driving a car begins to fade. Memories of childhood and adulthood begin to melt away. Personality changes become more apparent.

5. **Moderately severe cognitive decline** The person is unable to recall basic details such as their current address, their phone number, or the name of the sitting president. There is confusion about where they are or what year it is. They may say strange or nonsensical things, which is the onset of a condition known as dementia. People at this stage can still live independently, but will require some amount of care.

6. **Severe cognitive decline** A person may recall almost nothing but their own name. They may or may not remember the names of people closest to them. They tend to wander or become lost. They often need help going to the bathroom.

7. **Very severe cognitive decline** Recognizable speech is gone, although a coherent word may occasionally be uttered. People cannot walk, eat, or smile. Muscles become rigid.

It should go without saying that attempting a Homemade Biography will likely be a doomed effort if the subject has already crossed beyond the fifth stage. And even at the earlier stages, you may not have much time remaining to extract a personal history that you can completely trust.

One of the hallmarks of the disease is the patient's tendency to blend actual memories with irrational fantasies, or conflate two separate memories into one, or believe that an event seventy years in the past actually happened yesterday.

This presents a dilemma for the biographer, who is then put in the uncomfortable position of trying to separate fact from fiction in an event they never witnessed and from a time in which they did not live. The person being interviewed may insist upon the truth of a bizarre version of events.

How can you avoid upsetting your relative, while at the same time keep false information out of the permanent record? I spoke about this dilemma with Lisa Gwyther, education director for the Bryan Alzheimer's Disease Research Center at Duke Medical Center. She is also the author of *Caring for People with Alzheimer's Disease*. Gwyther suggests the following strategies for this difficult exercise:

DON'T EXPECT PRECISION: Specific details such as places, dates, and names may become confused in the person's mind, particularly after the third stage. If she tells you that she was married on June 10, 1953, for example, try to confirm that date with another family member or see if you might find it in a family document. If this is not possible—and if there is doubt as to the authenticity of the fact—you could try phrasing your hesitations in a gentle way in the biography. *Hester believed she was married on the afternoon of June 10, 1953. Recalling the event late in her life, she said she honeymooned with her new husband on the isle of Capri. No further details were available.*

LISTEN FOR REPEATED STORIES: Many older people have a habit of telling the same story over and over again, often to the very same listeners. (Perhaps, Reader, you're nodding your head right now with a mixture of love and annoyance). This habit is amplified in people in the early stages of Alzheimer's, but with a twist: New stories may emerge. The yarns may seem to be about banal things—a long-ago music teacher, the construction of a new highway, a sale on pantyhose—but there may be an underlying reason for the broken-record effect. "We have to assume that if people are repeating these stories, they must *mean* something to that person," observes Gwyther. And so you should therefore write it down. Once.

EXPECT CONFLATION: The mind has a powerful need to create meaning out of life's myriad events. This ability survives even into mid-stage Alzheimer's, albeit in a damaged form. What happens is that the person will remember only half a story and then blend it with parts of another story, either real or fictional. A story that starts with a trip to Chicago in 1944 to see the White Sox play baseball might end up with the speaker recounting details from a really exciting football game. You're not sure what's incorrect here—the stadium or the memories of the game, or possibly the whole thing. You can be certain, though, that none of it is a deliberate lie, only a jumble of disparate memories yoked together. They have been sorted this way by the mind's unconscious and incessant need to provide explanations about the world. Alzheimer's sufferers who do this "are trying to fill a hole with pieces that don't fit together," says Gwyther. In these cases, it is best to go only with what you strongly suspect to be the nub of truth in a jumbled story. Use neutral phrasing if you have to (see above). *Robert recalled going with his father to see a professional sports event in Chicago in the spring of 1944.*

DON'T GET OFFENDED: The sense of decorum that keeps our rude thoughts at bay often goes out the window at stage four. And so if you hear your mild-mannered relative suddenly saying nasty and provocative things about you or somebody else, I urge you not to take it too seriously. Chances are excellent that they don't really mean it. It is just ordinary grousing that would normally have been checked and repressed. You must also brace yourself for being called a different name than your own; second husbands are sometimes called by the name of the first, children are mixed up, and so forth. In these situations, you must remind yourself that the person you see in the chair in front of you is not who they "really are." That person would almost certainly be mortified if they knew what they were saying.

BE PREPARED FOR UNPLEASANT DISCOVERIES: That filtering device which keeps rude statements from emerging may be permanently shut off, as with someone who is drunk. This factor is known as *disinhibition.* It represents a gradual loss of the ability to distinguish between what's appropriate in conversation and what is not. And what might come out may not be just insults, but actual facts—the kind you may not want to hear. There is no guarantee that your subject won't inadvertently spill something they've kept hidden for years. "Any reminiscence has the potential to be rich and meaningful, but it also can be threatening," warns Gwyther. "We have seen men who call their wives by the names of a mistress. It's because the ability to plan out what you're going to say has been irrevocably lost. If something like this happens, you as a family member may have to piece it together." The line of repressed bad memories may extend all the way back to childhood. Female Alzheimer's sufferers who were sexually abused as children have been known to curl into balls when men enter the room.

KNOW WHEN TO QUIT FOR THE DAY: The mechanics of plaque interference is not well understood, but it is clear that mid-stage Alzheimer's patients tend to fade in and out of coherent states. This is what is meant by the old saying "good days and bad days." If you have caught your subject on a bad day, or if mild dementia is getting in the way of a productive exchange, simply squeeze their hands gently and come back again on what will, you hope, be a good day. But come back soon.

USE THEIR FAVORITE WORDS: The withering of language skills forces Alzheimer's patients to use only words in which they are certain of the meaning. You can help conversations go easier by repeating the phrases they keep favoring. Example:

Q: *So where did you like to go shopping?*
A: *Betsy liked the place with the hats.*
Q: *The place with the hats. That sounds like a nice store.*
A: *It was a place with a lot of hats in there.*
Q: *The place with the hats must have been close by.*
A: *It was on the corner. Nearby.*

Q: *The place with the hats. I'm not sure I know the name.*

A: *Frizell's. I think that was the name.*

DON'T ASK TOO MANY QUESTIONS: One of the many cruel aspects of Alzheimer's disease is that its victims can feel themselves slipping away piece by piece. And thus it becomes a matter of personal embarrassment when they are asked a basic question that they cannot answer. You may not intend your inquiries to come off this way, but people with Alzheimer's will sometimes view questions as insults to their declining powers. This can quickly put them into shutdown mode. "They view it as a test and see it as demeaning," says Gwyther. "They *know* that they once knew." She suggests that you phrase your questions as neutral statements and hope that your subject takes the bait. When fishing for a name, for example, try to approach it indirectly.

Q: *I remember hearing that your sister Edna was married before she met Bob.*

A: *Yes, I think so.*

Q: *I never learned his name.*

A: *Yes, I know.*

Q: *He must have been quite a guy. Edna's first husband. A very short marriage.*

A: *He was the pharmacist. Man named Taylor.*

Q: *Taylor.*

A: *Yes, Taylor. He was a drug addict.*

TALKING WITH VETERANS ABOUT
THEIR WAR EXPERIENCES

The freedom you have to read this book, or just about any book, came at a high cost. Part of that price might well have been paid by the old man sitting across the table from you.

In this section, I am going to use masculine terms exclusively to describe your subject, not just because the vast majority of America's combat veterans are men, but because of the unique role that warfare plays in the male psyche, particularly masculine tendency to repress inner horror. Few men who see combat can be unaffected by it, and nobody who hasn't witnessed it can ever understand what it is like to steal the lives of total strangers, and to see close friends die horribly, in an instant, and know that it was only luck that kept it from being you. These thoughts have to be planked underneath. To dwell on them is to go crazy. But the price is high for the survivors. A comprehensive 2002 study from the Yale School of Medicine found that combat veterans suffer from clinical depression and alcoholism twice as often as men who never fought. It may be that women will one day be deployed onto battlefields in greater numbers than today, but for now, this remains a generally male experience.

If a war veteran in your family has been reluctant to speak about his experiences, it could be because combat is much more terrible than most civilians can grasp. It is confusing, terrifying, and brain-searing work. It is also full of shame and self-hatred, no matter what the propaganda says. No motion picture has ever depicted its fullness. The historian William Manchester was part of the invasion force on Okinawa during World War II and he wrote about what he saw in the memoir *Goodbye, Darkness*. A portion is worth quoting at length: Manchester's first recorded kill. An experience like this may be only one of the horrors that your relative is unwilling to revisit.

Not only was he the first Japanese soldier I had ever shot at; he was the only one I had seen at close quarters. He was a robin-fat, moon-faced, roly-poly little man with his thick, stubby, trunk-like legs sheathed in faded khaki puttees and the rest of him squeezed into a uniform that was much too tight. Unlike me, he was wearing a tin hat, dressed to kill. But I was quite safe from him. His Arisaka rifle was strapped on in a sniper's harness, and though he had heard me, and was trying to turn toward me, the harness sling had him trapped. He couldn't disentangle himself from it. His eyes were rolling in panic. Realizing that he couldn't extricate his arms and defend himself, he was backing toward a corner with a curious crablike motion. My first shot had missed him, embedding itself in the straw wall, but the second caught him dead on in the femoral artery. His left thigh blossomed, swiftly turning to mush. A wave of blood gushed from the wound, then another boiled out, sheeting across his legs, pooling on the earthen floor. Mutely he looked down at it. He dipped a hand in it and listlessly smeared his cheek red. His shoulders gave a little spasmodic jerk, as though someone had whacked him on the back; then he emitted a tremendous, raspy fart, slumped down, and died. I kept firing, wasting government property. Already I thought I detected the dark brown effluvium of the freshly slain, a sour, pervasive emanation which is different from anything you have known. Yet seeing death at this range, like smelling it, requires no previous experience. You instantly recognize it as the spastic convulsion and rattle, which in this case was not loud, but deprecating and conciliatory, like the manners of the civilian Japanese. He continued to sink until he reached the earthen floor. His eyes glazed over. Almost immediately a fly landed on his left eyeball. It was joined by another. I don't know how long I stood there staring. I knew from previous combat what lay ahead for the corpse. It would swell, then bloat, bursting out of the uniform. Then the face would turn from yellow to red, to purple, to green, to black. My father's account of the Argonne had omitted certain vital facts. A feeling of disgust and self-hatred clotted darkly in my throat, gagging me. Jerking my head to shake off the stupor, I slipped a new, fully loaded magazine into the butt of my .45. Then I began to tremble, and then to shake all over. I sobbed, in a voice still grainy with fear: "I'm sorry." Then I threw up all over myself. I recognized the half-digested C rations beans dribbling down my front, smelled the vomit above the cordite. At the same time I noticed another odor; I had urinated in my skivvies. I pondered fleetingly why our excretions become so loathsome the instant they leave the body. Then Barney burst in on me, his carbine at the ready, his face gray, as though he, not I, had become a partner in the firm of death. He ran over to the Nip's body, grabbed its stacking swivel—its neck—and let go, satisfied that it was a cadaver. I marveled at his courage; I couldn't have taken a step toward that corner. He approached me and then backed away in revulsion, from my foul stench. He said,

"Slim, you stink." I said nothing. I knew that I had become a thing of tears and twitchings and dirtied pants. I remember wondering dumbly: Is that what they mean by "conspicuous gallantry?"

You—and not this book—will be the best judge of whether you should hazard a discussion about wartime experiences with a relative. Every ex-solider has complicated feelings on the business of killing. There is no universal method of talking about it in the "right" way; every man has his own timing. With any luck, by this point in the biography, and in your relationship, you've learned quite a bit about your subject's emotional life and his preferred methods of telling stories. You'll be uniquely able to pick up those nonverbal signs that will telegraph to you if he has any interest in talking about his time in war.

This may well be a discussion that you will never have. But I urge you to at least make the attempt. Do not let the fear of a shutdown deter you from a potentially valuable conversation. Odds are excellent that, provided you ask with respect, the mere motion of asking will be appreciated. It is also not uncommon for an old warhorse who has been silent for decades to suddenly find his voice late in life and begin speaking about events and images he has shut away for years. So many passionate things in a man's heart, even an old man's heart, often go unsaid for want of the right listener at the right moment.

This section is about becoming the right listener, and doing it with dignity and good feelings. I spoke about this with a few experts, among them Keith Armstrong, a licensed clinical social worker who is also a professor of psychiatry at the University of California–San Francisco. He is also a counselor at the Fort Miley Veterans Administration

Hospital and the author of *Courage After Fire*, a handbook for helping combat veterans readjust to peacetime.

Clear the room.

Find a time for this discussion when no other relatives will be around. Make things quiet and comfortable, with no noise or distractions. Block off all the time you think you need, and add an hour. *Turn off your cell phone.*

Make it not about them.

Many old soldiers remain tight-lipped because they don't want to be seen as making themselves out to be heroes. This may come from a version of survivor guilt, said Armstrong. His friends were gunned down, but he survived, and may harbor the belief that he doesn't deserve to grow into old age. One strategy you might try is to turn this section of the biography into a roll call of your subject's fellow infantrymen. Say something like "I think those men you served with would want their stories to be told. I'm interested in those guys. I don't want to see their stories just fade away." If you lay out this motivation, it moves the project away from self-aggrandizement and toward the traits of self-sacrifice and loyalty bred into all military men. And don't forget: Friends are mirrors for the self. This avenue of talk will trigger anecdotes not only about the subject's army buddies, but, more than likely, the subject himself.

Make it about the future.

You can further appeal to a selfless motivation by making it clear that the point of the exercise is to keep memories alive for future generations. "You could say, 'I really want my own children to know about this part of your life,'" says Armstrong. Other examples include "I want to be able to tell my own children about what their granddad/great-granddad did for their country" or "I want future members of this family to know about what it means to defend the nation."

Don't try to get it all at once.

Consider keeping the tape recorder off for the first half hour or so. Don't even take notes. You can go back over the details later. Create an atmosphere of relaxation and feel out just how loquacious your subject wants to be. "You want to find out if the water is warm," says Armstrong.

Show respect.

This probably seems obvious. But it bears elaboration. If you're familiar with the New Testament, you know the passage where Jesus tells his disciples not to cast "pearls to swine." What he meant was that they should be careful not to share precious spiritual insights with those who will only laugh at them; however, the proverb has a secular application as well. There is nothing worse than feeling that our inner wounds have been trivialized by an idiot listener. Most of us have had the experience of confessing a difficult matter of the heart to another person and then seeing indifference or distraction in their face. The urge to share hardens into a tough little ball. You berate yourself for trusting. Your secret now feels cheap.

Don't ever let this happen to a combat veteran. Whatever else may occur, you must respect him.

Forgive them.

Try to relieve the burden of guilt that many veterans carry around by making it clear that your feelings about them will not change, no matter what you hear. Their reluctance to talk may be rooted in the fear of judgment that comes with admitting that one has taken a life. Try saying, "No matter what happened in the war, I know the man in front of me is a good man. His whole life shows that to me."

A good question to keep things moving.

If a story rambles and seems to have no natural wrap-up, try asking "What did you learn from that?" It is a natural human trait to search for meaning inside upsetting events. Your subject might have some insight.

Watch for nonverbal signals.

Twitching hands, eyes that won't meet yours, reddening face. We all know how to tell when a man is starting to get upset, and when might be a good time to say after a long pause, "Would you like to keep going?"

Don't be too quick to stop.

At the same time (and I hope this doesn't sound too contra-dictory) don't immediately close the curtain on a hesitant vet. Give him the room he needs to decide whether he wants to risk a disclosure. This is where copious amounts of silence between your statements will serve you well. Let him turn off the tape recorder, if it will make him feel more comfortable.

Don't pretend to understand everything.

Avoid statements like "I know how that must have felt," if you weren't there. Use language of a more nondirective nature, such as "That must have been bad" or "I can't imagine how that felt."

Avoid political arguments.

Maybe you feel Truman shouldn't have dropped the bomb on Hiroshima, or that Nixon was too much of a coward in Vietnam. You can introduce that topic when the tape recorder is off, or with somebody else. Your focus now should be on one man's experience, not larger social contexts. Feel free to voice your thoughts diplomatically if your subject asks, but try always to lead the focus back to specific happenings. Opinions are much easier to come by, and are less interesting.

Wrap it up well.

Make it clear that you feel it is important to talk about these things, and you're glad that he did so, or at least made the effort. If it feels appropriate, make it clear that you love him. Leave the door wide open for future discussions of the topic, but only if he wishes.

UNCOMFORTABLE REVELATIONS

Combat is only one of many experiences your subject may be reluctant to talk about. Here's a story from fifteen centuries ago that illustrates a difficulty you may face when plumbing any sensitive territories in your subject's past.

At the height of its early glory, from 527 to 565, the Byzantine Empire was the most advanced civilization on earth. Its emperor Justinian I was a brilliant military tactician as well as an enlightened ruler when it came to matters of law and culture. He is best remembered for revising and expanding the old Roman legal code, parts of which still exist today in the Western legal system.

Unlike other strongmen of the time, Justinian had a talent for listening and taking advice. He packed his royal court with some of the best and brightest people of the region and took regular counsel from his friends, deferring to their expertise on some matters but flexing his own will when it suited him. Best of all, his wife Theodora was known for her street smarts, sense of humor, and unwavering support of his husband's policies. The emperor's energy and capacity for work was legendary; under his leadership, a vast array of castles and fortifications were constructed on the eastern frontiers. The empire's capital at Constantinople became known as the glory of the urbanized world, with the magnificent Hagia Sophia cathedral, built under the emperor's own sponsorship, at its center.

Much of what we know about him comes from a writer named Procopious, who was a legal aid to one of Justinian's top generals. He began writing a comprehensive account of the empire's military activities that eventually went to eight volumes. Procopious also wrote about advances in architecture, daily life in Constantinople, and Justinian's swift response to a plague that, at its height, killed up to 5,000 people a day in the capital. He became the foremost historian of the Byzantine Empire and his public writings are full of admiration and reverence for his emperor, as well as praise for the beauty of Theodora.

That was the official story, brought to us by Procopious.

More than a thousand years later, in 1604, some priests came across a long-forgotten document buried under a stack of scrolls in the library of the Vatican. Procopious was soon identified as the author. These writings were called the *Anecdota*, or "unpublished composition," but soon became known as the *Secret History* after it was published to great public fascination in 1624. And what a history it was! It was a salacious account of the hidden goings-on at Justinian's court, which Procopious had been too afraid to mention in his lifetime. The *Secret History* tells us that Theodora had grown up in poverty, begun working as a prostitute and a part-time actress, and that Justinian had fallen in love with her after watching her star in a lowbrow comedy. Procopious also confesses that the worshipful portrait of the emperor that he had set down in his "official" accounts was deliberately colored to make his boss look good.

I'm relating this story from Byzantium because I think it makes a useful illustration for the way that we all have a double view of our own pasts. Each of us keeps a "secret history" of the lives we have led, a private memory of all our failures and shortcomings and the things we've done that we're not so proud about—things that would mortify us if they were to be fully exposed to the light.

What exactly does our secret history contain? Freud called it the "dynamic unconscious." Poet Sylvia Plath alluded to "the terrible fish" that swims under placid surfaces. Anthropologist James Frazer dubbed it "the man inside the man." Literary theorists have called it "the double." Saint Paul makes this unforgettable complaint: "I see another law in my members, fighting against the law of my mind, and captivating me in the law of sin."

However you want to label it, the vast majority of

neuroscientists, philosophers, and theologians throughout history have agreed that a vein of animal impulse is threaded through every human being and that we will never quite understand the full power of this instinct. The ongoing struggle between the inner primate and the outer gentleman is an essential part of what it means to be human. Rage, greed, pride, lust: Each of these urges squirm inside of us, held in check by the heavy hand of self-control. I guarantee you that the relative sitting across the tape recorder from you keeps their own scrolls tucked inside.

How then should you handle it if your great-grandmother should suddenly confess to you that she always secretly hated your great-grandfather and took revenge by cheating on him repeatedly? Or if your uncle should tell you that he embezzled a quarter million dollars from a long-ago business partner and got away with it? Or if your grandfather should suddenly break down crying as he admits to being molested as a child?

As with so many other situations you may encounter in this project, there is no one correct response. But there *are* some general guidelines that can help you navigate rough waters with decency and dignity. I spoke about this with Dr. Anne Speckhard, an associate adjunct professor at Georgetown University and a widely published expert in the field of post-traumatic stress disorder, and with Dr. Peggy Roth and Dr. Kimberley Flemke, family therapists in private practice in the Philadelphia area.

Recognize the person's right to be heard.

Even if it makes you uncomfortable, you owe it to your subject to sit and listen. The process of a Homemade Biography is, above all, one of self-discovery and your subject has reached a point where they feel you deserve to see the un-pretty side.

Relax.

Maintain eye contact. Don't look away; this might reinforce the sense of shame you're trying to dispel. Ease your body to avoid giving off any nonverbal signs of discomfort.

Stop taking notes.

Don't create a feeling of exploitation. If the person is un-comfortable with the tape recorder, turn it off. You can de-cide later, in partnership with your subject, how much of this should go into the finished product.

Don't react too quickly.

If you're tempted to be disgusted with your subject, re-member the French proverb: "To understand all is to for-give all." Every misdeed, no matter how inexplicable, has shadings and logic behind it that no mortal can ever hope to grasp in full. Know that you're hearing only a tiny frag-ment of a very complicated story, and reserve judgment. The last person who needs to be judged right now is your subject; they have judged themselves more harshly than you ever could.

But do react eventually.

Long silences and nothing else might be interpreted as in-difference. If stuck for something to say, try a neutral state-ment: "I'm really honored that you felt comfortable enough with me to start talking about this. I know it must not be easy to revisit this after all these years."

Wait for more.

It is likely that you will get bits and pieces of the story before you hear the complete version. This is a common way for people to make a confession they feel is shameful. "They are going to test you," said Speckhard. "They may be willing to tell you everything, but they have to test you first." The way you react to the first gambit will play a big role in their decision to talk.

Prompt gently.

If the topic involves a known family scandal or tragedy, Flemke suggests you address the topic indirectly by saying "I am interested that this has never come up in all the time I've known you. Why have we never talked about this before?" Or Roth's version of the same thought: "This seems like a really hard subject for you. What is it that makes it tough to talk about?"

Avoid eagerness.

Whatever you do, don't act like you just *have* to know. The urgency may be off-putting.

Emphasize the survival.

However bleak the episode, the person got through it somehow. This might be the best way to approach a sensitive subject—it is more about overcoming the adversity rather than the adversity itself. Passing on this hard-earned wisdom to others is one of the best ways a person can create a redemptive "story" around their hardship. Their suffering was not for naught, because it can serve as instruction for others. Try venturing something like "I'd like my grandchildren to know about the strengths that were inside this family. And one of the best strengths in life is learning how to deal with events beyond your control."

Touch gently.

A light hand on an arm or a knee might go a long way. But it also might not be appreciated by a certain type of stoic. Your judgment, of course, will be the world's best on the matter of to touch or not to touch.

Stay fixed in time.

Let the story unfold in chronological order. Jumping from point to point will make them unnecessarily nervous. Always build on their last statement. "And then what happened after that?"

Don't get in the way.

Resist the temptation to say "Are you really sure you want to talk about this? We don't have to." Although your motivations come from a good place—you want to make them feel comfortable and give them an easy out—they will hear it as a signal that they have made a faux pas. Say instead "I am interested in listening if you want to talk more."

Don't feel guilty.

It may not seem like it at the time, but you are probably doing your relative a tremendous favor. Putting words to the unspoken is a good thing in itself. "When they talk, they are creating a narrative for themselves," said Speckhard. The unhealed have never done this." So you must remember that a lot of good is likely being accomplished. Unless you've been rude or pushy, you have nothing to feel sorry for.

Consider who they've been hiding from.

The sense of shame that may accompany a disclosure is often the remnant of a social façade that was constructed for the benefit of people who are long dead. Your subject may be still playing a role for a theater that emptied years ago. This is one more reason to be generous with your forgiveness.

Go back again.

If a story seems emotionally false or tied up too neatly in a package, you might consider fishing for more. Speckhard suggests asking this question: "Is that the whole story?" Or: "Is there more there?" Or in cases where pain is obviously being suppressed and the smile is fake: "Was there a sad side of that for you?"

Ask good follow-up questions.

"What was helpful in this situation? What wasn't helpful?" This relieves the focus on the painful event itself, and takes it into the realm of how the person changed because of the incident. It may also yield some revelations of its own: the unexpected kindness or cruelty of a friend or relative, the introduction of a new figure in your subject's past, the surprising ways that your subject has coped with disaster.

Psychoanalyze with care.

It now may be crystal clear to you that your grandmother divorced three times because she was neglected as a child. But pause a moment before suggesting this out loud. Ask yourself: Will it be received well? Is the person self-aware enough to appreciate the insight? If you think the speculation is important enough to actually go in the manuscript, make sure the subject agrees with your conclusions.

Empathize.

Repressions come from a universal human feeling: the shame of *not having been good enough*. In their minds, they failed somehow. This is the root of most secrets that people keep. They have been protecting themselves with silence or compartmentalization, perhaps for decades. In talking, they risked embarrassment and rejection. They deserve respect.

Stay awhile.

This will sound like the most obvious piece of advice ever given, but you shouldn't leave the person's side right after a major revelation. Have a glass of wine. You've both earned it. Make sure they know how valuable it was for you to have talked about difficult things. Let them know that the door is not closed, that the topic can be revisited if they wish. Don't worry about whether it should go in the manuscript or not. Decide that on next visit, after the person has had time to reflect.

WHEN THINGS GET PERSONAL

Here's one unique part of doing a Homemade Biography that few therapists would have to encounter. No ethical therapist would ever work with a relative; you don't enjoy the luxury of professional distance. And so there may be occasions when a traumatic family subject comes up in conversation and *you* are personally involved.

It might be something as upsetting as the death or disappearance of a person close to you; or an annoyance, like having to listen to you or your parents criticized or demeaned; or a troublesome development, like the blatant recasting of an event in ways that you know are at odds with reality.

Before you respond, Speckhard advises you to take a moment and weigh your ability to talk neutrally about the subject. If you feel in that moment that you would be unable to separate your feelings from the matter, then you ought to remain silent. Change the subject as soon as you can. Hard conversations may take place inside the interviews for a Homemade Biography, but it should not be an arena for exchanges that have a probability of wounding the relationship between yourself and the subject. A good rule of thumb: If it feels like it will probably get ugly, steer clear.

If this remains uncertain, however, or if the discussion

promises a better understanding of the past, Roth suggests you edge forward with this question: "Would it be helpful if I talked about what that experience was like for *me*?" Unless you've talked about this previously, you should not assume the subject has ever considered this.

As always, the air in the room should always be suffused with friendliness and a sense of shared adventure. If you feel you are being pressured to go along with false versions of history, or have to listen to things that are personally demeaning, you have little choice but to end that particular line of conversation and segregate that material from the finished manuscript. It is the ethical thing to do. You'd simply be too biased to write a straight account. Walk the high road without any fanfare (if you have to have fanfare, it is not the high road) and shift the focus back to the parts of the person's life story in which you have no direct role.

A ONE-SHOT?

One reason why many attempted biographies fizzle is the sheer lack of time to have a complete series of conversations. This isn't necessarily anybody's fault, particularly if you happen to live on the other side of the country from your subject and see them only rarely. An incomplete or rushed project can make the subject feel frustrated. But it would be much better to take down a small amount of material rather than have the person die with none of it down on paper and the memories forever lost.

Following is a brief guide for compressing the interview portion into a single afternoon. Make sure it is your *only* option before proceeding.

The "first session," covered in Chapter 2, should now be

considered your only session—or, at least, the only one you may have. Think of the few hours you'll have as an extreme acceleration and compression of the general plan laid out in this book. There won't be much room for entertaining tangents and relaxed banter, unfortunately, as you will have to stick to a schedule.

Here's how it should be organized:

HOUR ONE: Turn on tape recorder. Brief small talk before moving into the timeline. Important names, places, and dates written down in chronological order on the legal pad.

HOUR TWO: Move back to subject's childhood and ask for key anecdotes. Ask about anything you've never quite understood about your subject's upbringing or family circumstances. Guide them toward adulthood with prompts from the timeline (for example, "So then you moved to Michigan and went to college?").

Be sure to ask most about the things you *don't* already know. Covering familiar ground, as fun as it may be, would be a waste of time under these circumstances.

HOUR THREE: Cherry-pick a few questions from Chapter 5, especially the ones you think might yield an unexpected answer from your subject. Even in this rushed format, you don't want to shut yourself out of the surprises that a Homemade Biography can bring.

Finish by resolving not to finish. Go home and write it up, but make it clear to the subject (and yourself) that you'd like to amplify things at a future date. This will reduce their sense that they've just dictated a death-row testament, and it should also be an encouragement for you to improve on what you've been able to learn in these hours. You can't predict how many future holidays you may have together. There may be more; this might be the last. Said the Spanish writer Fernando de Rojas five hundred years ago: "No one is so old that he cannot live one more year, or so young that he cannot die today." This remains true.

A FINAL THOUGHT

I had always known that Grandma had married twice, but I understood very little about the death of her second husband, Fred. A picture of him sat on the coffee table: He had a Tab Hunter haircut, wore a dark suit, and had soulful eyes like big olives. He was leaning to the right and forward, as a lounge crooner would lean toward a microphone. My mother had told me vaguely that he had died of a kidney disease when she was a teenager.

To say the circumstances of Fred's death was a "forbidden" subject would be too melodramatic, but it certainly was not a subject that was ever discussed in my presence when I was growing up. Pieces of the story filtered down to me over the years: I came to learn he had not died of a kidney disease, but had shot himself to death one night after suffering a bout of depression. Still, the details remained hazy.

I knew the subject would have to be addressed with Grandma in some fashion, but I was reluctant to bring it up. After all, it was a horrifying chapter in her life, as the gunshot death of a spouse would be for anyone, and I wasn't sure if she would want to make any elaboration upon the bare fact. Not knowing how to proceed, I asked her daughter to take a temperature reading.

Her daughter, of course, happens to be my mother,

Joanne. They have a standing date for a phone conversation every Saturday morning.

My answer came back in a week: "She says she's willing to talk about that with you," said Mom.

"So it's okay to ask about the suicide?"

"She says whatever you want to know, feel free to ask."

I won't forget what I learned about my step-grandfather during that session. Fred had grown up in tough circumstances with four brothers in an orphanage outside Chicago in the 1920s. He was a loner and an autodidact who read the encyclopedia for fun. When World War II came along, he was of draft age and was trained in explosives. His unit was deployed to New Guinea in 1944 to help clear the island of Japanese troops after the American invasion. This was to be among the most savage fighting of the entire war. There were almost no accurate maps of the terrain. The jungles were mazes of mountains, swamps, and near-impenetrable groves of trees. Entire columns of Japanese troops were sent in to defend the forest and abandoned there; later rescuers found evidence of cannibalism among the lost and starved soldiers. American troops nicknamed the island "Green Hell." Fred was out in the jungle one day with a lieutenant on a mission to defuse land mines. Their jeep hit one of the mines, they flipped upside down, and the lieutenant was killed. Fred lay wounded and pinned under the jeep for several days with the dead man at his side. Nobody knew where to find him in the chaos of combat, and it was likely he had been given up for dead. The lines shifted while he was trapped there, and Fred played possum while Japanese troops streamed by the overturned jeep. If he had moved or coughed, he would have been slaughtered. Fred was eventually pulled out by an American platoon, but that was the end of the war for him. He was sent to a service hospital in

San Francisco and diagnosed with a mental disability before his discharge.

My grandmother Ann, who met him four years later, didn't find out any of this until much later in their marriage. He would never discuss what happened in the war and she had to hear bits and pieces of it from his brothers. Their courtship had been quick, in any case: Fred had come to Phoenix on vacation after the war and met my grandmother in a neighborhood bar. She was recently divorced, the mother of an infant girl, out of a job and out of sorts. Phoenix was looking a lot like . . . well, you already know about that.

Fred professed a passionate love for her and she grabbed onto him tight. They married in a border town in Mexico three months later. He moved into my grandmother's house and took work as a draftsman, and later found even better jobs in the booming postwar Phoenix economy. My grandmother got pregnant and gave birth to a son. Fred built them a new house on an unsettled piece of desert land the family had claimed free from the government. And it seemed like a good match except for one thing. Fred always said he suffered from a case of "malaria" he picked up during the war. He claimed this was the reason he often could not make it out of bed in the mornings. But this was no virus: It was undiagnosed post-traumatic stress disorder, largely unknown in those days. He suffered for thirteen years before his eventual suicide.

This is the section of my grandmother's biography that deals with it (slightly edited for style):

> *He was having increasing difficulty sleeping and was out of a job. The last day of his life, September 26, 1960, he spent working on "Henrietta," the red Studebaker. Ann*

said, "The night he died, he couldn't sleep. Up and down. I went off to sleep with Joanne. And later, I heard the shot. I knew what it was immediately." She called War- ren, the deputy sheriff [her brother] and told him "no sirens." The deputies cocked their guns and went in with flashlights. Warren came out and said, "He's gone."

There was no note. Ann believes he was acting on a mo- mentary impulse of despair and that it was not a planned decision.

As I've said, it would be going too far to call my step-grandfather's suicide a "family secret," but it never came up in any conversation that I did not initiate. My mother al- ways thought it was not worth dwelling upon, and certainly nothing that would be good for a child to try to understand.

I think many family skeletons are like this—not "secrets" in the classic sense, but events that everyone has stopped talking about out of a sense of decorum. There is no active repression or intentional distortion of the truth, only a miss- ing spot in the past that comes from an oversized sense of politesse. Nobody wants to be the rude one to bring it up. And so it lies there buried under a layer of inertia.

Grandma, too, came from a line of hard-handed Ap- palachian coal miners who had gone to the desert to raise cotton and work as police officers. They would have rather swallowed a bag of nails than have complained about their lot. Her late husband was clearly not a talkative man when it came to personal pain. It is no surprise to me at all that his suicide was a closed subject for decades. But I am very glad I learned of it, and I believe Grandma was glad she revisited the story. We did not dwell overlong upon it and no blame was assigned to anyone. But we finally did talk about it.

I never met Fred, but he is a more real person to me for this experience. He fought for his country and endured a darkness that took his life. He was an uncounted casualty of World War II. That his suicide seems to have been a desperate reach for a cure makes him all the more human to me, and real. Later generations will know that he was not a bad man.

I believe it is better to confront the tough events rather than let them sit in respectful ignorance. A sanitized version of the past is not what you set out to write. Silence is a lie all its own. The truth can be difficult, but there is beauty in it.

CASE STUDY

Listening Carefully

There are two extreme types of interview subjects and—thankfully—most people fall at some point in between.

At one end of the spectrum is the "Raven," who, like the bird in the famous poem by Edgar Allen Poe, gives only one-word answers to any question you ask, refusing any enticement to be more colorful or expansive. *Nevermore* is all you get.

At the other end is the "Ancient Mariner," who, as in the famous poem by Samuel Taylor Coleridge, grabs any nearby listener by the shirt and jabbers about his life until he nearly collapses from exhaustion.

Lori Lefkovitz, who passed along the "Ancient Mariner" comparison for me, is a professor of literature at the Reconstructionist Rabbinical College in Philadelphia. She encountered both types of people when she started asking questions about her own family's history. This would prove to be more difficult than it sounds, as her family had been traumatized by the Holocaust.

Many of Lefkovitz's relatives—particularly her father, a survivor of Auschwitz—had told their stories to professional interviewers over the years and were well accustomed to taking that mental journey back in time. Lefkovitz didn't do a biography of her family in the precise spirit of this book, but she has listened to her father's stories of the Nazi death camps over the years and wrote about it in an essay for the *Kenyon Review,* published in 1996. She reports that her father was an uncorkable storyteller of the Ancient Marnier variety:

> My dad, like Coleridge's sailor, is most concerned that we get the point of the story, see it his way; he doubts that he has told it well or told it all. He wishes we would listen, wonders why he has never been able to tell us that which he has told us a thousand times. He asks me to watch his video testimony. I do, and I praise his recall, and I tell him that there is nothing there that I have not heard before. He's not convinced, and he is sure he has left out important details, and he is annoyed with himself because he does not remember everything. So I ask about his three younger siblings murdered in the gas chambers. To his chagrin, it takes him a day to remember one of their names, and he is unsure of their ages or the color of their hair.

In many ways, this is a gift for an interviewer: a person who has a burning desire to tell the story of their life correctly and completely. There's rarely any need to coax them. They'll tell you everything you ever wanted to know, and a lot that you didn't want to know. They want you to *feel* the story the way that they felt it. Which is impossible.

So how do you handle this type of interviewee with sensitivity, particularly when the story they have to tell is so central to their essence as a human that it demands the utmost respect?

The best thing you can do, says Lefkovitz, is to just sit back and listen and be comfortable with the idea that you might be able to empathize with a portion of it, but you can never truly understand exactly what the person experienced or how it made them feel. And you should not attempt to feign total understanding. Pretending to "get it" when you don't is a lie that should never be told, because it breaks the bond of trust that must exist between you and your subject. On some fundamental level, our deepest experiences are lonely ones. We can try to talk about them, make sense of them out loud, describe them in vivid color, write them down, repeat them over and over, and our listeners still really wouldn't grasp the thing entirely.

You have to accept this limitation in your own project. But you must still listen with patience. Because in a Homemade Biography, the person will often start off talking with the purpose of making you understand, but will wind up talking mostly to themselves so that *they* will understand. The stories may seem remote and inscrutable at first, but give it time. You will find yourself becoming the silent enabler, the pass-through, the wire through which the electric current travels. Lefkovitz reports she began to feel like a ventriloquist's dummy in the course of hearing her parent's stories. But out of that odd experience came a gift: a better understanding of herself and of life in general, albeit an unusual comprehension.

"What came into clarity for me was the depth of my own ambivalence toward my own family's history," she concluded. "Everything I value in life was made possible by the Holocaust. Had life gone smoothly for my parents and if they had stayed in Europe, and even if through some miracle they had found each other, I never would have been born into the miracle that is America."

She goes on to explain in her essay:

> In the world that was destroyed by Nazism, my parents would have been an impossible match. He a village Jew, ethnic, not devout; she from Polish cities, with some prestige, ritual slaughterers, rabbis, circumcisers, and her own mother had studied art and piano in Germany. Class, nationality, religiosity, ethnicity, education, ideology— everything imaginable—separated my mother from my father. But in 1948, both survivors found themselves in Brooklyn, and when they found each other in the early 1950s, no marriage seemed more natural to their friends and family. Survivors both, they emerged from a fire that had had a democratizing effect on the Jews; it leveled the ground. And out of a union that would have been fantastically bizarre in pre-war Europe, come I.

You may be seeing this effect in your own project already. Nobody who attempts a Homemade Biography will finish it without developing a new conception both of themselves and of the amazing complexity of life. I don't think it's an accident that the "Rime of the Ancient Mariner" ends with its focus not on the old sailor but on the nearly invisible listener he has been talking to for hours.

> *He went like one that hath been stunned,*
> *And is of sense forlorn:*
> *A sadder and a wiser man,*
> *He rose the morrow morn.*

Writing Techniques

Now comes the time when you're going to sit and write it all down. I have good news for you. It's easy. Much easier than you think.

It's going to be easy because you're going to skip a step that can make your life miserable. I strongly recommend that you not transcribe your interviews. In other words, I don't think you should play all your tapes back to yourself and copy down every word that your subject uttered. That's a recipe for boredom and drudgery and eventual surrender. A very good typist takes three hours to transcribe each hour of tape; an average person will need five hours. There's an entire day down the tubes, for just *one hour* of conversation. What you get at the end is often ten percent interesting and ninety percent chaff. And if you want to convert the good stuff to a narrative version, you're in for even more typing. Double the work, half the fun. Forget it. There's a better way.

This book advocates a technique I used when I was a

newspaper reporter. It was useful on tight deadlines and helped relieve a lot of the stress of writing. When I started writing my grandmother's life story, I slipped into it almost without thinking. It's nothing unique to me—no trademark or patented process here—and I'm sure that many of the writers and reporters down at your local paper have used a version of it at some time or another. If you've written for a living, you might have used it yourself at some point. I call it "instant composition."

Here's how it works. Find your timeline and your tape recorder. Seat yourself in front of the computer and open up a blank page. At the top, write a basic sentence like this: *Henrietta Jacobs was born on March 24, 1927, during a snowstorm in Marquette, Iowa.* You'll have the exact date and town on your timeline. The snowstorm bit you know by heart from the interviews. It is very important that this sentence be factual and ultrasimple, because it will set the tone for everything to follow. Do not put any adjectives or anything else descriptive in there just yet. Don't be tempted to call it a "raging" snowstorm, or say it was a "quaint" town. The words may seem dull and unadorned, but you must not worry about that.

The first lines in my grandmother's bio were these: *She was born November 10, 1915, at the Deaconess Sister's Hospital at Van Buren Street and 3rd Avenue in Phoenix, Arizona. It was three years after Arizona had shed its territorial status and become the forty-eighth state.* These opening words were like the first turnings of the wheels of an aircraft as it speeds down the runway, gathering pressure under the wings that would eventually send it aloft.

Find the spot in your tapes where your subject talks about the circumstances of their birth. If you didn't talk about that, zip around until you find their first memories. The key is to go as far back in their life chronology as you can. Don't worry about their ancestors or their parents—that will come later. The beginning of a Homemade Biography is always the beginning of your subject's life.

Now it's time to fly. Push PLAY on the tape recorder and start typing *fully formed* journalistic sentences using the information coming from your subject's mouth. You will be essentially weaving your own sentences together as your subject speaks. Think of yourself as a loom: You take cotton in one side and process a blanket out the other. It requires a bit of practice at first, and you will make a lot of mistakes at the beginning, but trust me—this is much easier than it seems. In time, you will be making sentences at the exact speed that your subject is talking. It is by far the most efficient way to get your subject's life on the page, without the dull business of transcription.

See this example:

On the tape

Q: Tell me about how you were born.
A: It was on March 24 in the year 1927.
Q: Where were you born? In Muscatine?
A: Well, it was inside the farmhouse.
Q: Not in a hospital?
A: No, very few families could afford that in those days. We had a midwife named Clara Johnson who did a lot of business in the area. She knew my folks pretty well and when the time came for me to be born, my mom told me this later, Clara rode twenty-four miles on horseback to our house. There was a spring snowstorm that night and Clara wandered off the trail a few times, but she

made it just in time. The labor went pretty quickly. I was the eighth and last child and Mom was used to childbirth by then. She probably could have done it on her own. [Laughter]

What you typed as you listened to the tape

> *Henrietta Jacobs was born on March 24, 1927, near the town of Muscatine, Iowa. It happened during a snowstorm. She was delivered by a midwife named Clara Johnson who did a lot of business in the area. Few families could afford hospitals then. Clara rode twenty-four miles on horseback to be there that night. She wandered off the trail a few times but arrived just in time. The labor "went pretty quickly," said Henrietta. Her mom was so used to giving birth "she probably could have done it on her own."*

Notice a few things about that example. The sentences come at the tempo of the subject's recollections, one right after the other, the facts stacking up in logical order. They aren't the loveliest sentences ever written, but your goal is not to win the Nobel Prize in literature. Your goal is to preserve an account of the life of your subject in plain language. Imperfections in the prose can always be ironed out later, which is one of the many benefits of writing on a computer. It takes only a few seconds to burnish a flat sentence into a livelier one. *She wandered off the trail a few times* will become, in very short order, this: *She wandered off the trail in the blinding snow, but made it to the house just as Henrietta's mother was ready to give birth*. But save that editing for later. Keep going; don't stop.

This method works even if you're a slow typist. If you find it initially difficult to keep up with the tape, try getting just the "stub" of the sentence down on the page. Don't concern yourself with the King's English; you can fix that later. Misspellings are irrelevant, too. Take down the gist. Here's how the above example might play out in this "quick form":

Henrietta Jacobs was born on March 24, 1927, during a snowstorm in the town of Muscatine, Iowa. (Remember, that's the sentence you calmly typed with the recorder off; now here comes the raw stuff.) *Dilvered midwife Clara Johnson, couldn't afford hospital, rose 24 miles hourseback, labor wnet pretty quickly, "she proly could have done it on her own."*

It looks terrible on the page, but it will be quite easy to smooth it out later.

If you're a plodding, four-fingered typist like me, it can be difficult to keep punching in the quote marks. It takes a second longer than it should; you have to push SHIFT with one thumb and find the "and" with another. Here's a trick: Just use the capital Q on the front end to signal a direct quote, and then trust your instinct to know when the quote ends. Here's how it looks at first:

Michael was police officer with san diego, used to petrol beach, frequent contact with surfers and their girlfiens. QHe always said he couldn't believe some fo the thigns they used to bring on theoir picnics. Also parotled Balboa pk before being transfer to detective.

This eventually becomes:

Her cousin Michael worked as a police officer for the city of San Diego. His first job was on the beach patrol, where he had frequent contact with surfers and their girlfriends. "He always said he couldn't believe some of the things they used to bring on their picnics," she said. He also was responsible for patrolling Balboa Park before he was transferred to the detective bureau.

Needless to say, you should feel free to hit the PAUSE button to let yourself catch up with the tape. Also, you shouldn't hesitate to hit the REWIND button if you have reason to believe you got a major fact wrong. It is best not to sweat the small stuff during this instant composition phase, however, as the chances of an error making it into the final product is almost nil, as we will soon see. So you shouldn't fuss over the unpolished sentences, half sentences, stubs, run-ons, misspellings, and grunts pouring forth from your fingers. The last thing you should do is agonize over the quality of the writing. Perfection is not your friend. In fact, nothing kills a Homemade Biography quite like perfectionism. You must free yourself to create writing that is merely simple, nothing more, because at the end of it all, you'll see how beautiful it really is.

Now comes a reality you must face: You will need to set aside at least two good workdays to get your subject's reminiscences down on the page in this crude form. My own debriefing took a little over fourteen hours in total; I had about ten hours of tape from Grandma. That's a rate of about ninety minutes of typing for every sixty minutes of tape, and I'm not even a very fast typist. Yours might go faster if you didn't tape as much as ten hours. It will obviously take longer if your conversations were lengthy. Your eyes may be a bit glassy and your shoulders may ache a little before it's over. But, again, there's some good news attached: Once you're finished with it, you never have to listen to those tapes again unless you really want to.

I recommend you save them, however. Label each one with a little piece of masking tape and type up a brief note explaining what they are for someone who stumbles onto them a hundred years from now. It might look like this:

> ### FAMILY ORAL HISTORY
>
> *Lisa Langley talks with Henrietta Jencks*
> April 2, 2007—May 19, 2007
>
> Tape A—Birth and childhood
> Tape B—School and marriage
> Tape C—Marriage and children
> Tape D—Reflections on life

Put the tapes and page (perhaps along with notes and photographs) in a metal box. Store it in a place where it won't be misplaced, and safe from the elements. This could be one of the best gifts you may be able to give to people whose parents have not yet been born. Imagine what it would be like to hear the voice of your great-great-great-great-great-grandmother. Perhaps she would have a story to tell about playing hide-and-seek during her childhood that would make her sound familiar.

The heavy lifting is now finished. Now comes the easy part.

THE STYLE

A teenager joined the reporting staff of *The Kansas City Star* right after he graduated from high school in 1916. He was the son of a doctor from the wealthy Chicago suburbs, and had no apparent interest in going to college. Family connections helped land him the job on what was then one of the most prestigious newspapers in the nation. Ernest Hemingway was a bright kid with a sharp eye, but his writing needed work. He liked baroque sentences laden with emotion and overwrought with description, and this simply wasn't going to fly at the *Star*, which was in the business of telling its readers the news in a straightforward way. A city editor named Pete Wellington handed Hemingway a booklet that would change his life: *The* Star *Copy Guide*.

The opening lines were: "Use short sentences. Use short first paragraphs. Use vigorous English. Be positive, not negative."

These admonitions could just as well be carved over the door of every newspaper in America. They also function as excellent guiding principles for the writing style of your Homemade Biography.

Hemingway stayed at the *Star* only nine months before finding his way to the World War I battlefields, but he later credited *The* Star *Copy Guide* with helping him develop the literary style that would revolutionize American letters. "Those were the best rules I ever learned for the business of writing," he said later. "I've never forgotten them. No man with any talent, who feels and writes truly about the thing he is trying to say, can fail to write well if he abides with them."

It's true. There is no way you can fail to write well in this project if you follow the simple rules Hemingway picked up in his apprenticeship at *The Kansas City Star*. Your sentences should be like railroad cars. They exist for only one purpose—the hauling of cargo. Your words are bins designed to carry information to your reader. Don't worry about whether the words are beautiful or not. Their beauty is in their function and their simplicity; they will be elegant like Shaker furniture. Or a wooden kitchen spoon. Or a freight train (I love freight trains). Here are a few lines from my grandmother's biography, chosen at random:

> *Evan was a bit of a troublemaker as a kid. Once he and some friends greased the rails of the streetcar near an incline and laughed as the streetcar spun its wheels. In later life, as a Phoenix cop, Evan once got called out to a service station at Polk and Grand to investigate a kid stealing pop from a machine. It was the same service station where he used to steal pop himself. Ann invited her hairdresser Bunny to come live in the house on Polk Street with her and Evan. Bunny, a blonde with big breasts from Mesa, worked at a salon on Van Buren between 14th and 15th Avenues. They became close friends, wearing look-alike dresses and double dating. "We thought we were just the cutest." Downtown theaters in those days were the Fox, which had loge seats and where Wayne Newton, in his high voice, would later introduce the pictures, and the Orpheum, where the balcony was designated "colored," where Ann preferred to sit. One regular date: Jimmy Llewellen, a good swimmer.*

Yes, that's *the* Wayne Newton, a kid from Phoenix who later made it big in Las Vegas. I threw him in there as a *Forrest Gump*–type detail. The mention of him, like almost everything else in this section, is part of a chronological river of raw data with very little artifice; nothing more than chunks of basic information speckled with the necessary articles and prepositions to make it readable. I had asked Grandma to give me a few recollections of her time as a recent high school graduate in postwar Arizona and she had told me about Evan's rail-greasing adventures and Bunny's big breasts and the matching dresses and Jimmy Llewellen, all in that order. And that's how it went down in the biography, with a little *Kansas City Star* style to make the sentences compact and digestible. I wasn't striving to create Shakespearean couplets or call the birds down from the trees; I was out to tell Grandma's story, nothing more or less.

And so when you're sitting at your computer, weaving those taped conversations into instant sentences, I encourage you to swing your words like meat axes. Chop with blunt strokes. This is no time to get fancy. Use simple sentences and don't agonize over them for a second. Let subjects and verbs be your best friends. Keep it simple and keep it short. And above all, keep it going.

> *The family moved to New York City in 1954 after Peter's father was discharged from the army. Their first apartment had two rooms. It was located at the corner of 68th and York, in a neighborhood that Peter's father hated because it was so far from his welding job at the Brooklyn Organ Pipe Manufacturing Co. There was a diner down the street with big glassy windows where the three of them ate every Sunday after church. Peter always had the same thing, eggs and pancakes with boysenberry syrup on the side.*

The heart of good biography comes down to filling ore cars with raw fact and pushing them on down the rails.

Even the worst writer in the world will be graceful with this approach.

SOME REVISION TRICKS

After you've done the instant composition and finished all your tapes, you should have a running stream of facts flowing in chronological order, from your subject's birth until the present moment. You should go back over it once more, smoothing out awkward patches and adding sentences that make it all hang together.

In the numerous cases where you've written a line like *blt house dte back from road, once acre, sycamore tres, Qit was ht e nicest piece of land wwe could find in theat part of arkron*, you'll of course want to iron it out into *They built the house set back from the road a good distance, on a one-acre lot with sycamore trees. "It was the nicest piece of land we could find in that part of Akron," she said.*

There are a few more turns of the wrench you can make to tighten up your prose, and I'll relate them here. But don't treat them as dogma. The key to editing is just the same with writing: Don't sweat it too much. Nitpicking can be hazardous to your health. Always favor productivity over perfectionism.

Smooth the jump from thought to thought

Add a "transitional sentence" at the tops of paragraphs or between disjointed thoughts. It most often will be a restatement of the obvious from the facts you've already laid out, but it'll help the reader process the information more easily.

Example

> *He would hitchhike between Birmingham and Huntsville to see Elizabeth each weekend that summer. She was a student in a business college there, and was learning to be an accountant. His boss at the mill fired him in September when the price of steel dropped and he had to take a job as a garbageman.*

> *He would hitchhike between Birmingham and Huntsville to see Elizabeth each weekend that summer. She was a student in a business college there, and was learning to be an accountant.* THEN HIS OWN CAREER TOOK A TURN FOR THE WORSE. *His boss at the mill fired him in September when the price of steel dropped and he had to take a job as a garbageman.*

Instantly reformat your words into graceful sentences

Build a vigorous subject-verb construction at the beginning, and then "bend" it off into whatever direction you desire with the aid of a word bridge such as "who," "that," "which," "many," and so on. Roy Peter Clark of the Poynter Institute calls these "right-branching sentences."

Example

> *Mike's bar was a rough-edged place, with holes in the gypsum-board walls, sticky floors in the bathrooms, an ex-con nicknamed "Weezer," who did bouncer duty on Fridays, and an address that the cops knew well from their frequent visits to break up fights, often triggered by*

arguments over the sports betting that raged in the back-room when the Seahawks were playing.

Notice how the sentence took a bend after the first comma. We have the vital information immediately up front with a strong subject and verb ("Mike's bar was . . ."), and can then back-load the sentence with as much color and detail as we please.

Make sentences flow into each other

Repeat a key word or concept from the first sentence in the second, and so on.

Example

It rained on the day they were married. The National Weather Service said it was the heaviest rainfall that Kalamazoo had seen in six years, but it didn't ruin the wedding. The Jacksons simply moved the wedding inside the recreation hall at the park, and asked the priest to lead their vows on the volleyball court.

See the subtle repetition of the root word "rain" in the second sentence? It's a way of building a nearly invisible bridge in the reader's mind between one sentence and the next.

Capture a little of your subject's own voice

Simply stick quotation marks around some of your speaker's exact descriptions, and especially their colorful turns of

phrase. Don't worry if it's only a fragment; you can para-
phrase the rest of the sentence yourself.

Examples

*Mike didn't invite her to the wedding "and that just set
my teeth on edge," she remembered.*

*The company had been pinned against the mountain
ridge by the enemy line. "The bullets were coming down
on us like rain," he said.*

*"Their chances were slim to none, and Slim had done left
town," he said of his prospects for college.*

*Mother said the dress made her look "like a hog wearing a
rainslicker," but Anna thought she was being too modest.*

Be stingy with adjectives

They have tremendous power, and the most powerful thing
they often do is ruin your writing. Note the following sentences:

Rachel clapped a hand over her mouth.

*Rachel clapped a terrified hand over her trembling
mouth.*

Both lines convey the same information, but the second
one makes us wince with its overstatement. Too many of
these and we begin to lose faith in the writer's honesty. Adjectives generally do not add power to the writing—in fact, they

strip it away. You'll be surprised how much of the adjective's meaning is actually contained in your unconscious choices of verbs and nouns (the word "clapped" conveys quite a bit, for example, in the sentence above). There are exceptions. A *single* well-chosen adjective does occasionally have power to juice up a sentence. But as a rule you should be parsimonious.

Same goes for adverbs

Think of them like Tabasco sauce. A tiny shake every now and then is good. Too much and you ruin the dish.

Know how to use a semicolon

It is an excellent tool for this kind of writing because it connects two complete sentences with a discreet seam. Think of it as a "soft period." Do not use it to connect run-on sentences together.

> WRONG: *After school, he worked in the drugstore on the corner of 4th and Main; homework neglected at the insistence of his boss, Mr. McTavish.*

> CORRECT: *After school, he worked in the drugstore on the corner of 4th and Main; his boss, Mr. McTavish, would not let him do his homework on the job.*

Avoid clichés

"Her heart beat like a drum." "She saw her life pass before her eyes." "The baby was as cute as a button." Yuck. If you've heard the phrase before, try not to use it. Aim to surprise the reader with new comparisons and similes.

Details

Remember "the name of the dog and the brand of the beer" you asked about during the interview phase? Don't forget to sprinkle those details throughout your account. They build authority in the text and breathe life into the events. For example: *Her father was watching an episode of* I Love Lucy *when she interrupted him to say she would be marrying Bob the next week.*

Fill in details for the uninitiated

Assume that most people who read your manuscript— particularly those five hundred years from now—might not automatically know that Ethel's son was killed in Vietnam or that Salem was a vanishing small town about eight miles from the county seat. Read your manuscript over to make sure that you haven't unconsciously slipped into jargon or assumptions that would be confusing to an outsider.

Don't dwell too much on logistics

Too many writers waste everyone's time describing the order of a person's actions in getting from place to place. It's annoying in novels when we have to read about the protagonist opening the door, turning on the light, crossing the floor to the kitchen, etc. So it goes here. Unless it provides an illuminating or entertaining story, you need not spend time in the manuscript pushing your subject down streets or through hallways. Hide the dull motions and the reader will fill them in unconsciously.

A FEW WORDS ON STRUCTURE

Like the lives they portray, biographies generally start at the beginning and move forward through the years. There are a few exceptions to this rule. Psychological studies, academic papers, and certain experimental biographies will sometimes guide the reader through somebody's life using an idea or an intellectual concept as its pulley rope. But the best propulsion device yet invented is *time*. Your project, like nearly every other biography ever written, will almost certainly be of the "this happened, and then that happened" school of storytelling. Start at the person's birth, move through the events of the person's past in sequence, and end with the person's present.

There are many virtues to this approach. It is clean and easy. It is a natural organizing principle for a tangle of facts. It unfolds like life itself. And best of all, it will be instantly accessible to your reader, which is your top goal. Remember that you're writing this document not for just you and your subject, but for those family historians (and unknown people rooting through attics) who will be reading your work centuries from now. It would be best not to confuse them with too many narrative devices and linguistic tricks. Straight-forward chronologies won't go out of style, even in the year 2234. So unless you really want to try an avant-garde style of telling your subject's story, I recommend you stick to a basic sequential narrative.

That said, there are still some simple ways you can tinker with the architecture to create a certain effect. I'll use a fictionalized example to highlight a few:

Anecdotal lead

Start with one of the best stories you heard, and then move into the subject's birth.

Example

One of the most surprising moments in Matt Eckstrom's life happened when he was forty years old. It was the fall of 1964, and he had been teaching shop class at Western High School on the edge of a tough neighborhood in Sacramento for the past five years. He had been wondering if it might be time to leave what he felt was a dead-end job. One Saturday morning, Matt started up his cash-green 1948 Mercury, revved the engine, and heard a sound that he described as "a death rattle." It was the telltale sound of a piston coming loose from the pin and breaking through the engine block. Matt opened the hood and surveyed the damage. "My God, it was a disaster in there," he recalled. "A real mess, but I didn't want to give up the Mercury. That car had a lot of sentimental value for me." But repairing an engine block is a difficult thing to do—it is like the heart surgery of auto maintenance. Matt was very gifted with mechanical talent and had made a career out of teaching kids about cars, but he didn't trust himself to do it properly. So he called for a tow truck and had the car taken to one of the better grease parlors on the south side. The manager of the place was a tall and muscular young man who greeted him warmly and said, "Hey, don't you recognize me, Mr. Eckstrom?" It turned out to be Ronnie McManus, who had been a menace to the other teachers at Western High School ten years earlier. He had been suspended and arrested multiple times for vandalism and assault, and most teachers and administrators assumed that he was destined for a career stamping license plates up in San Quentin prison. But here he was, managing a reputable engine block shop, doing the kind of repair that not even Matt knew how to do, and talking to his customers like they were human beings. "You taught me most of what I know about cars," said Ronnie. He and Matt chatted a little bit longer and at the end of the conversation, Ronnie said, "Listen, Mr. Eckstrom. I know I gave you a hard time when I was a kid. I quit drinking and I now I'm married and have a baby of my own and things are much different." It was not an explicit apology, but it might as well have been.

"He didn't need to apologize to me," said Matt. "His life was proof enough that he had made a big change somewhere along the way. And what Ronnie was also telling me was that my role as a teacher hadn't been wasted, even though I was feeling like it at that point in my life. Most of the time, you never know what effect you have on people, but sometimes God shows you a piece of it."

This life full of helping people began on April 4, 1924, in the small town of North Bend, Washington, when Matt was born to a farm implement salesman and his schoolteacher wife. . . .

Thematic lead

Begin with the general theme of the subject's life, and highlight examples as you move through the years. See Chapter 6 on "Writing for Theme" for tips on how to isolate these life threads.

Example

Helping people has always been second nature to Matt Eckstrom. He started early, as a household helper to his mother. He then became a ten-year-old assistant to his father, who sold farm implements around the Pacific Northwest. He later went on to work as a bus driver, navy mechanic, school crossing guard, Sunday-school instructor, high school shop teacher, and drug and alcohol counselor. He now volunteers three times a week to read books to other seniors whose eyesight is not as good as his. In all of these jobs, and in his personal life, he gave of himself selflessly without any thought of repayment. "Most of the time, you never know what effect you have on people, but sometimes, God shows us just a little piece of it," says Matt.

He was born on April 4, 1924, in the small town of North Bend, Washington, the son of a farm equipment salesman and his schoolteacher wife. . . .

Flashbacks

If there was a pivotal moment in a subject's life, and if it bears relevance to the action at hand, don't be afraid to refer to it out of sequence.

Example

They rarely fought, but when they did, it was always memorable. It always came back to the same thing—her feelings that Matt was not taking a strong enough role in raising the children. One weekend, about nine years into their marriage,

*she blew her lid. "You never do anything unless I ask you!"
she said. "Why don't you take them out to baseball games, or
something? Take some initiative instead of always reacting."
It suddenly made him remember the casual remark Sgt.
Blakely had made to him that day by the docks at Hunter's
Point. "Stand up for yourself more, soldier!" Says Matt: "She
made me remember that lesson that I had to keep learning
and relearning my whole life, which was that people eventually get frustrated when you always let them take the lead. I
tried to bring that lesson into my marriage and in my approach to my boys."*

Historical furniture

Take a break between paragraphs to quote from a popular
song on the jukebox that year, mention who was president,
describe the men's fashions of the day, briefly relate what
was in the news, and so on. Think in terms of not just what
was happening in the world or in the country, but also in
the town where the subject lived. This can bring a sense of
place and time to your narrative.

Example

*At the end of the year, the school board voted in favor of
the tax increase and the new teachers were hired full-
time. It meant that Matt's job was there as long as he
wanted it. It also meant they could finally afford to move
across town to the westside. They bought a house at the
corner of 11th and K Street, a three-room house with a
swing set in the backyard and a persimmon tree in the
front.*

This was in 1953. Dwight Eisenhower had just been

inaugurated as president of the United States, promising that the nation would encourage "policies that encourage productivity and profitable trade." Ernest Hemingway won the Pulitzer Prize for The Old Man and the Sea. *The first issue of* TV Guide *hit the newsstands. The movies* From Here to Eternity, Shane, *and* Roman Holiday *were at the theaters. Chevrolet introduced the Corvette, which featured an aerodynamic windshield and a body made out of fiberglass. It was right before the dawn of rock-and-roll. The big songs on the radio were "How Much Is That Doggie in the Window," sung by Patti Page, and "Don't Let the Stars Get in Your Eyes," by Perry Como. In Sacramento, it was the time when the company Aerojet opened a factory on the eastside to build missiles and other defense equipment. Meanwhile, the famous "Sacramento 6" drive-in movie theater was flooded with customers, and not a small number of teenagers who used it as a make-out spot. The most popular post-movie restaurant on a Saturday night was Cookie's on H Street.*

Matt and his family liked their new neighborhood. . . .

How do you find this stuff? Very easy. Google will have it on your computer screen in thirty seconds. Any other good Internet search engine will do the same. Simply search on "America in (YEAR)" and let your fingers click across the decades. One excellent site where you might be directed is www.factmonster.com/yearbyyear.html.

Many American cities and towns also have their civic histories uploaded somewhere on the Internet, and you should feel free to select historical facts from them. I would caution you, however, not to appropriate anyone else's writing as your own. Plagiarism is a silly crime. There's just no reason for you to burglarize somebody else's candlesticks when you're perfectly capable of casting your own. Simply take the bare historical facts only—such as Dwight Eisenhower being inaugurated in 1953—and rephrase them in your own language. This rule does not apply, of course, if you are quoting somebody directly and giving them proper credit, as with the above example from Eisenhower's speech.

Be sure also to mention your research sources in a brief note at the end of your Homemade Biography. An appropriate note might say something like: *Information about the history of NASA was taken from the Web site www.spacecadet .net.* Even if you're not planning to publish your biography, it still is the proper scholarly thing to do. It's also good manners.

Now, with those caveats in mind, I want you to feel no fear whatsoever about inserting historical facts into your narrative. Nobody has any "copyright" on the events of the past. It is certainly *not* plagiarism simply to repeat the undeniable fact that Elvis Presley first sang "Hound Dog" at the Cotton Festival in Memphis on May 15, 1956. That data belongs as much to you and me as it does to Elvis.

If you prefer to do your research the old-fashioned way, your local library's reference shelf will yield a rich stock of material. In particular, these books provide good slivers of Americana arranged by year:

- *Timelines of World History,* by John B. Teeple (New York: DK Publishing, 2006)
- *American Decades* (Detroit: Thomson Gale, 1996)
- *Chronicle of America* (Mt. Kisco, NY: Chronicle Publishers, 1989)
- *Encyclopedia of American Facts and Dates,* by Gorton Carruth (New York: HarperCollins, 1997)

Withholding information

You'll need to be judicious with this next technique because it could potentially frustrate your readers, but one way to inject a little suspense into your narrative is to withhold a key piece of information for a few beats, just long enough to keep the pages turning. Let the scene play out as it did in life, when your subject may have been in the dark about an important development. Every life has its moments that are just as dramatic—and even as corny—as the movies.

Example

> Matt was working at the high school one day that May when the secretary called him over the intercom. He decided to finish his lecture about brake repair before responding. When he got to the office, the secretary told him that he should call home. There was "a certain look on her face," said Matt, but she would not respond to his questions. He called Susan, who told him there was an important message she had to give him.
>
> "Well, just tell me now," he said.
>
> "I have to tell you in person," she said. There was a strange high note in her voice, as if she was under stress.
>
> "This is silly," he said. "Just tell me."
>
> "I'll come pick you up after school." This was all she would agree to.
>
> He had to wait until the end of the school day. Part of him worried that one of his parents was sick, or had died, and that Susan didn't want to deliver the news over the phone. Was it one of her parents? Or could it be that something was wrong with the house, and needed repair?

When she showed up behind the wheel of his cash-green 1948 Mercury at the turnabout in front of the office, he slid into the passenger seat.

"Okay, what?"

She handed him a book about baby care and didn't say another word. He opened up the cover and inside the flyleaf were these words in her handwriting: WE'RE PREGNANT.

I think you'll agree it would have been a bad idea to have begun this anecdote about Matt's life with the sentence: *Susan chose to surprise Matt with the news of her pregnancy.* If you have a good suspenseful scene, don't give away the ending too soon.

Other voices

I said earlier that it is to your advantage to shoo other relatives out of the room when you're doing the interviews. But here's one corollary to that advice. You may want to consider sprinkling voices from other relatives throughout your Homemade Biography, as a counterpoint or complement to the main point of view (that of your subject). These other voices can function like sidebar commentary, and sometimes they can tell you things you would never hear from the subject themselves.

Example

Going into election day, Henrietta was confident of victory. She had campaigned especially hard in Brookhaven, the section of town closest to the river. She personally knocked on every door in that precinct and even spent *an extra $1,000 for extra yard signs to plant in the lawns of her supporters there. She cast a vote for herself at her usual polling place at the high school. "It was so strange to be there, where I had voted for every president since Harry Truman, and to see my own name on the ballot." She held a party at her house that night and about fifteen of her friends showed up. Not wanting to appear too eager, she sent Bob down to the county recorder's office to report the results, which would not be posted on the bulletin board until midnight. Everybody grew anxious as the hour grew late and a few people drifted away. Finally, at 12:20 A.M., the phone rang: It was Bob calling from the pay phone outside the courthouse. He asked to speak to Henrietta. "I could hear it in his voice before he told me the news," she said. She had lost by just twelve votes. Henrietta kept her composure as she informed her friends of the defeat. "Then I had a brandy and went to bed," she said. The next day was Wednesday and she reported to work as usual, with a calm demeanor. It was the last time she would ever make an attempt at public office. She kept only one yard sign and one handbill in the attic as souvenirs. Said Bob: "She refused to feel sorry for herself, but I know it really hurt her. She felt as though the town had rejected her personally. I think the worst part came a few years later, because time proved that she was right. We had a big flood in 1981. The rain came down for three days straight. The river overflowed in Brookhaven and the storm drains couldn't handle the load. Twenty houses had to be evacuated and the Red Cross even came down and set up a small shelter for those people at the Rec Center for a few days. There were about a dozen cots there on the basketball court for* *those people who couldn't find a relative to stay with. And Hen went down there and volunteered, serving coffee and whatnot. And she never said a word about that election, at least not in public. She refused to say I-told-you-so. That's just the way she is. That was the year the council finally agreed to get a bond issue going to fix the problem. A lot of people might have taken some pleasure in the whole thing, being shown to be right and all, but not Hen. She didn't want to remind people how they had rejected her."*

A cautionary note: You may want to consider interviewing these relatives separately and then running their thoughts past your subject in conversation before including them in the manuscript. Nobody wants to be surprised by alternative views, particularly those with which they disagree.

Don't forget the windows

Paul Rusesabagina, the Rwandan hotel manager, made a suggestion about writing that I've never forgotten. During one of our first meetings, I was making a drawing on a board, showing him my proposed "architecture" for his memoirs. I made a brief map of all eleven chapters and explained how they would naturally join into each other.

"It's a little bit like building a house—you have to pour a foundation, or it will not stand," I told him.

"But we must build windows into the house, too," he said.

"Windows?"

"Yes. It cannot be too serious in every place. There must be light and air."

He was exactly right. No person's life story ought to be a cheerless march through dates and names. Brighten up the atmosphere with an occasional digression or funny story. It will lighten the load for the reader and may help communicate something distinct about your subject.

Here are a few lines from my grandmother's story, with what I hope are a few good windows in the house. I am telling the story of her first job, which was working as a secretary in a Civilian Conservation Corps warehouse in Tucson.

The Clothing and Equipage division of the Purchasing and Contracting department consisted of three men and Ann. The boss was Harry R. Caulkins, a former furniture salesman from El Paso with a shiny seat on his pants. "The three guys used to kid me all the time. They said I had two rubber ears and I could stretch them out in any direction and pick up whatever I wanted to hear. It was kind of true. Boy, I really knew what was going on." Two of her colleagues were married, and the single one, Ray Hartley, had a beautiful singing voice. He dated her, as well as other women. They had a stormy romance, dating others and making each other jealous on occasion. "Those were the good old days and I didn't even know it," she said. Ray was not the first boy she had kissed. The first was on a doorstep after a junior-college dance.

She went up the south side of Mount Lemmon with Ray and a friend one time. It was a single-lane road, with designated hours for up travel and down travel. They went to a CCC campground that had just been constructed. There wasn't much to do on the mountain, so as a game they pitched pennies. Ann won and piled up the pennies and some pretty rocks on the picnic table. They had made coffee at the campground and she put them in the empty coffee can. They moved on to another area and had planned to go back and collect the pennies and the rocks, but the hour grew late and they had to leave because they didn't want to drive down the bumpy road in the dark.

More than a year later, Mother and two of her brothers came to Tucson for a visit and they went back up the mountain and to the same campground. There were the rocks and pennies in the coffee can, just where they had been left. They had been there all through the winter.

I love this passage for a couple of reasons. My grandmother has always been a lover of gossip, but hearing about her "rubber ears" when she was a young secretary puts it in a whole new perspective for me. The shiny pants seat of Harry Caulkins is also an amusing detail. Grandma has told that story about the Mount Lemmon pennies for years, and I was happy to get it down on paper, where the details could be memorialized forever. I remember going up that south back road when I was in high school and it is still in pretty rough shape. Those CCC campgrounds were brand-new in those days, and the fact that a can of pennies would be undisturbed for an entire year tells you something about the public's slow embrace of the improvements that the government was making to the Arizona backcountry in the 1930s. It is strange to imagine her going up Mount Lemmon with her pals in much the same way that I would take my own friends up the same mountain a half-century later (though we didn't brew coffee over a campfire). I wonder if this trip would have even been remembered, or discussed, if it hadn't been for the mildly amusing story of the pennies on the picnic table.

These are minor details to the story of her life, to be sure, but they make for nice windows.

Run it past the expert

I said earlier that you shouldn't worry too much about accuracy in the rough draft. Here's why. You'll be running your facts by the most expert fact checker of all: the subject. Ask them to review the manuscript for accuracy before you put it in final form. If they show reluctance to read it, or cannot because of poor eyesight, offer to read it to them. This virtually eliminates the possibility of publishing an error.

Very important: Make it loud and clear that this review is focused on the truth and nothing but the truth. In other words, you should encourage them *only* to correct wrong names and dates and other concrete details, not to nitpick about word choices, or your mentioning Aunt Glenda's divorce because Aunt Glenda might read it and get mad. If you suspect that the subject might get nervous all over again about a touchy subject, you can try avoiding that trouble with this extra step. Make a list (in private) of all the facts that you doubt and want to check. Then read to them *from that list*, checking as you go, and don't volunteer to show the manuscript or read it to them until the final copy is ready. There is no sense in creating unnecessary anxiety, especially if you have already had a discussion about the best way to handle sensitive material.

If an antsy subject specifically asks to see the rough manuscript, however, you have no choice but to show it.

At the end of the day, the story belongs to them. You'll just have to have that negotiation over Aunt Glenda all over again.

A LAST THOUGHT ABOUT "BAD" WRITING

Near the end of his life, the great American author Henry Miller told an interviewer at Big Sur, California, that he preferred writing that was raw and uncultured to writing that was beautiful. He said that the amateur stuff gave him the sense that he was seeing the true feelings of a man's heart, whereas the writing that was letter-perfect made him suspect that the honesty had been wiped out of the prose.

Miller said a similar thing on another occasion: "I believe when you write freely and easily and joyously, even if it doesn't make sense, that you do more good than when you write seriously with all your heart and soul and are trying to convince people."

One of the biggest temptations for any writer is to look at the words they've written and say, *Ugh, this stuff is el stinko*. And what usually happens is the writer then quits for the day to do the crossword puzzle, or do the laundry, or flip on the soaps while the manuscript languishes. And the book never gets written.

I encourage you to bid good-bye to any frustration with your perceived lack of talent. Because guess what, reader: you *are* talented. Both Ernest Hemingway and Henry Miller say so. Don't argue with those guys. Anybody who can make a simple subject-verb sentence, and stays true to their subject, cannot fail to tell a good story.

And the best story topic in the world sits with you at the Thanksgiving table—a human with a full life and many decades worth of great stories to share. You must not let your fear of "bad" writing get in the way of getting their story down on paper for future generations. Nobody then is going to care if you can't think of a good synonym for *laughed* or didn't describe a St. Louis neighborhood in the 1940s as vividly as you might have. The enemy of good writing is the conviction that you must be a good writer. The best friend of good writing is the freedom that you grant yourself to be a bad writer. There is great liberation in allowing yourself to be less than perfect.

I mean this sincerely: The only writing that really *is* bad writing is the writing that never gets put on the page.

Man, that stuff is *terrible*.

CASE STUDY

Baseball and a Buzzcut

Sarah Corrigan's assignment for a high school AP English class was to write a biography of somebody influential in her life. She chose her aunt Martha. And after only one interview with her aunt, Sarah produced a fourteen-page account that I think is an excellent example of biographical writing style. It is simple, informative, and very lightly stylized—that is, stylized just enough so that this brief story of Martha Moore's life has a certain arrangement and theme, but not enough that the reader is beat over the head with it, or where the facts obviously have been twisted to fit a preconception.

Martha's life was certainly one that made for a good story. She had grown up in a conservative Irish Catholic family and went to an all-girl college in a suburb of Boston. The cultural rebellions of the 1960s enchanted her and she hitchhiked to Oregon, where she renounced her Catholicism, protested the war in Vietnam, smoked pot, grew flowers, listened to experimental music, and lived as a hippie for six years. She married, divorced, moved back east, and now runs a plant nursery outside Sturbridge, Massachusetts.

Sarah chose to begin Martha's biography with the metaphor "life as a roller coaster." It may be a cliché, but it matters very little in this case. Sarah wasn't aiming to win an award for this piece of writing. Sarah's only goal was to be as clear as possible and to be faithful to the life experience of her subject.

The fact was that Martha *did* ride a roller coaster for the first time at the age of twenty and that it *was* a transformative experience for her, which helped influence decisions about her spiritual life that would change her destiny. Here are the opening lines of Martha's life story.

At the age of twenty, when Mary Martha Corrigan Moore rode a roller coaster for the first time, she did not die. She had been taught to fear roller coasters and their twists and turns, high points and low points, her whole life. She was led to believe that they were unsafe and posed too many risks to be enjoyed. So, she cowered from them for a while—until she threw caution to the winds and went on the ride of her life.

Mary Martha Corrigan came into the world on December 26, 1951, when Harry Truman was president, McCarthyism was on the rise, television was in its infancy, and the world was still recovering from World War II. She became the second child of Mary Patricia Quinn Corrigan, a secretary, and Matt Wilson Corrigan, an attorney and World War II vet. Little Mary, or Martha as she is henceforth called, grew up not unlike most other children of the time. She had two loving, middle-class, Irish Catholic parents who settled in the quiet Lynn neighborhood of Pine Hill. She had an older brother, James, a freckled kid with a buzz cut and a baseball. There was a

*clean sidewalk that ran perpendicularly to the blue Ply-
mouth Belvedere in the driveway and a large window in
the kitchen that overlooked a fenced-in backyard.*

There are a few things going on in these sentences that I want
you to see. Notice the clean and uncluttered way information is
delivered to the reader. We learn in the second paragraph the
date of Martha's birthday, the names of her parents, the location
of her first house, and a brief description of the family's historic
and cultural port-of-call, all in a straightforward way. Sarah does
make a few verbal flourishes, but these sentences in the second
paragraph are good sturdy boxes full of hard information. This is
the red meat of any Homemade Biography. Fact is everything.
Stylizing comes later. In fact, to some degree, the best style is no
style at all. The bare facts may provide you with all the style you'll
ever need.

I'll go further: fact *becomes* style, if you know how to dispense
it right.

Sarah provides us an excellent example of this at the end of
the second paragraph. Martha's brother is a "freckled kid with a
buzz cut and a baseball"—a vivid and economical sentence bearing two well-chosen details. I think any fiction writer would be
proud of that buzz cut and baseball. They furnish an instant mental picture of this 1950s kid. Sarah was able to capture this verbal
snapshot from an actual snapshot: a photograph of her father as a
young boy, complete with hair and horsehide.

The next sentence is even better, to my way of thinking. That
"clean sidewalk" that runs "perpendicular to the blue Plymouth
Belvedere" is another deft stroke of the word-brush. Anyone familiar
with America knows the look and feel of this suburban street, even
if they've never been to Massachusetts. That sidewalk could have
been just a "sidewalk," but Sarah decided to make it clean. Almost
unconsciously, the reader knows what Martha's well-scrubbed

childhood home might have looked like. And the image of straight lines evoked by the union of sidewalk and blue car foreshadow the rigid borders of a postwar suburban lifestyle that Martha will soon trespass. This effect was accomplished not with gimmickry but with the graceful reportage of information.

In later paragraphs, Sarah makes sure to weave in some information about the national attitudes and tastes that would shape her aunt Martha's life. The following passage contains a bit too much generalizing for my taste, but it still provides a good example of mapping a subject's life in the context of larger societal trends. Notice the way the sentences lead into each other.

She began to socialize with kids from other public nondenominational high schools. They were from the wrong side of town, and the trends they were following got the best of Martha's curiosity. They were up to their ears in Vietnam War protests, civil rights protests, and anything else that they passionately believed in that would separate them from their parents. Their hair was far out, their guitars were groovy, their clothes were psychedelic, and their message was peace, love, and happiness for all. The hippie generation had arrived.

Hippies had a mission. They wanted the world to let go of possessions and wealth and be reintroduced to a simpler, happier way of life. Whatever they had, they shared. They embraced other cultures, other religions, and had an open mind regarding almost everything. Martha wanted that lifestyle; she was ready for it. She had found her outlet and her voice.

The gears of this passage work smoothly because the sentences are both easy to digest and full of color. We begin with our primary subject—"She"—and move quickly into how she collided with the kids with their new ideas and fashions. These are not necessarily short sentences, but they are still simple and strong and easy to follow, beginning with a subject ("they") followed immediately by a verb ("were") and trailing into a string of descriptors ("psychedelic," groovy," "peace") that, while a bit facile, still manage to fix the still-evolving Martha into a definite place and time in American history. This type of writing is what will make for compelling reading for Martha's descendants a hundred or two hundred years from now: the true audience of a Homemade Biography.

By now, we can see the arc of Martha's life developing. She has embarked on a journey away from the values and religious faith of her parents and started following other roads.

Living with her parents again made her even more restless and there was so much to see and do. Hitchhiking was ideal. Back then, it felt safe to just stick out your thumb and be thankful for what the motorists shared with you. Food, water, even a place to stay could be trusted and so Martha took advantage of it. She decided to go to the source of all the action. New England was too familiar and it was time for a serious change. Martha went out to the West Coast and led "a charmed life." No worries, no stress, just pure and natural living. Martha eventually hitchhiked six hundred miles from Portland, Oregon, to San Francisco, California, alone.

What we don't get here, of course, is a sense of what Martha's parents thought of all this. The omission is noticeable, but not necessarily fatal. It is important to remember that your biography will be focused on just one person—the protagonist, you might say—and all the friends, lovers, family members, co-workers, enemies, and others in their lives are supporting players. They will inevitably be of great interest, and perhaps worthy of their own cul-de-sac digressions in your narrative, if only to make it clear why they were so important in your protagonist's life. But the loudest voice *must* belong to your subject. Just as we hear our own thoughts the loudest from day to day, a biography should reflect the echo chamber of your subject's mind and nobody else's. A choice could have easily been made to query Martha's parents on how they felt about their twenty-year-old daughter hitchhiking to Oregon—and it would have made a welcome addition in the writing—but only inasmuch as it did not rip the main focus away from Martha. It would be relevant only if it was relevant to Martha.

Remember that roller coaster image Sarah began with? We return to that image at the very end.

Martha feels she is beginning to explore death herself through the aging process. She still leads the simple, back-to-nature life by not wasting energy and refusing to use household and garden chemicals. She doesn't have any plans to color her hair or take hormones, anything that fights the inevitable. Martha hopes to leave this world gently and quietly without struggle, and she looks forward to what's next.

Martha is not facing death, but she has been around many that have, including her beloved father, Matt, who died at age seventy-six from a stroke. At age forty-nine, Martha believes life is a brief separation from God, or Nirvana, or whichever higher being one believes in. Death is a natural process, Martha believes, and people should embrace and explore it for as much as they can get out of it and by example, show others left behind.

"All my life experiences have taught me not to fear death [says Martha]. With all the crazy chances I have taken, I know that someone has been watching out for me and will continue to" . . . even while on roller coasters.

The closing quote is the only time Martha's unfiltered voice is heard in the course of the document. This was a different approach than I took in my own quote-laden biography of my grandmother, but that doesn't make it wrong. It represents only another approach, and probably came about as a result of the way Sarah interacted with her aunt. Her source material consisted of a letter from Martha, as well as a lengthy telephone call. The call was not tape recorded and Sarah didn't write down many direct quotes. Her main focus was getting the raw information.

You'll see that the image of the "roller coaster" circles back to us in the context of Martha's journey toward finding a belief system that gives her peace. Martha's spiritual road turns out to have been the spinal column of her life, as well as—naturally—the central theme of this biography. Sarah captured it on the page and was true to her subject. That automatically makes this project a successful one.

9

Taking It Further

There is no natural end to a Homemade Biography. Every person contains a miniature world humming inside of her or him, no matter how little they show on the surface, and you could talk and talk for the rest of your lives without grasping even a fraction of that mini-world. At some point, though, you have to know when to call it "done"—as done as you can reasonably make it—and commit this project to the shelves.

One of the most important holy books in Judaism, the Talmud, says that anyone who saves a single life has saved the whole world. You may not have literally saved a life with this project, but you *have* saved some irreplaceable memories of that life. And that is deserving of respect. This chapter is about how to safeguard those memories with class and care—and how to use technology to leave something extra for future generations.

FILLING OUT THE FAMILY TREE

Some of the conversations you've had with your subject have doubtlessly been about other members of the family— perhaps people you've never met. Now might be an ideal time to start plugging that information into a basic family tree, if you haven't already. It makes an excellent graphic companion to a Homemade Biography and provides an easy key to some of the characters who will crop up in the narrative.

The first thing you need to know is that this isn't nearly as hard as it seems. You have numerous tools to use. The science of genealogy—a word from Greek meaning "the study of descent"—is one of the oldest and most commonly practiced types of history in human civilization. It may be the most basic type of history known to man. Memorializing one's ancestry is important to the politics, economy, and religion of nearly every culture on the globe. European kings used this discipline to prove their right to the throne. They drew up elaborate charts showing the tangled branches of their lineage connecting to previous rulers. Wars could hinge upon a disputed link in the family chain. The ancient Israelites held the line of descent in spiritual esteem; their scriptures are full of "begats." Jesus' own genealogy receives special attention in the New Testament. The rulers of pre-colonial Hawaii chanted a complicated series of verses called an *oli* that named their distant ancestors in song, and helped legitimize their claims to various pieces of land on the islands.

But genealogy, like biography, is a pool of water with no bottom. We may all come from a common set of parents, but none of us can reach back with either memory or documents into the beginnings of mankind. That has been hidden from us. The castlines into our origins will always trail off into nothingness at some point, whether at the Domesday Book or just at great-grandpa Ted who may have come from Ohio, we think.

What this means for you is that your genealogical probing can be as deep or as shallow as you want it to be. This section is not meant to serve a comprehensive guide to creating a family chart, but rather as an overview to the basic tools at your disposal. Here's a list of instruments, resources, and places you might find helpful in documenting your subject's biological provenance.

Pedigree Chart

This is the elementary building-block of genealogy. You might find it particularly useful for a Homemade Biography because it focuses on only one person. It looks like one side of an NCAA Final Four bracket, with the subject listed as the "winner," with the parents branching out from them, each parent with their own parents branching outward and exponentially into the infinity of the past. They usually stop after four or five generations, but this is a triangle with no hard right side. The vital data that accompanies each person on the chart include: name, date of birth, place of birth, date of marriage, date of death, and place of death. Many Pedigree Charts have holes in them (missing dates, places, or even names), in which case you just fill in "unknown." Because the Pedigree Chart is concerned with siring rather than relationships, the multiple marriages and divorces that pepper most family trees are not included. Everybody is the blended DNA of just two people, which is the only information the chart seeks. Free downloads are available at www.familytreemagazine.com.

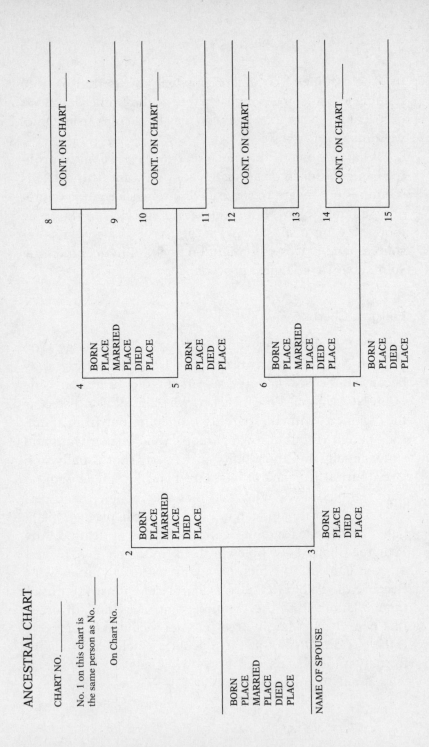

ANCESTRAL CHART

CHART NO. _____

No. 1 on this chart is
the same person as No. _____

On Chart No. _____

2
BORN
PLACE
MARRIED
PLACE
DIED
PLACE

BORN
PLACE
MARRIED
PLACE
DIED
PLACE

3
NAME OF SPOUSE

BORN
PLACE
DIED
PLACE

4
BORN
PLACE
MARRIED
PLACE
DIED
PLACE

5
BORN
PLACE
DIED
PLACE

6
BORN
PLACE
MARRIED
PLACE
DIED
PLACE

7
BORN
PLACE
DIED
PLACE

8
CONT. ON CHART _____

9
CONT. ON CHART _____

10

11

12
CONT. ON CHART _____

13

14
CONT. ON CHART _____

15

Family Group Sheet

This is the other major document you'll find useful. Though much of the data points are the same as in a Pedigree Chart, its primary focus is on the family unit and not the individual. The Family Group Sheet is especially useful for keeping track of siblings. In ideal circumstances, your Homemade Biography will include three genealogical documents: a Pedigree Chart for the subject, a Family Group Sheet in which they are listed as a child, and a Family Group Sheet in which they are one of the parents. Your subject will be the best place to start for help in getting the document filled out initially. There will inevitably be some holes that you may have to plug on your own (more on that below). Free downloads can be found at www.familytreemagazine.com.

Bibles

The Bible is full of genealogies and one of them might actually be yours. For families in eighteenth- and nineteenth-century America, it was standard practice to record the names, birthdays, marriages, and deaths of the kinfolk in the blank front pages of the family Bible. The Bibles themselves were large ornate affairs, designed to be more like heirlooms than study manuals. This habit of noting vital statistics in the foreleaf has been a boon to amateur genealogists. Ask your subject if there's a family Bible somewhere in the house.

Attics

Old photographs, high school yearbooks, birth certificates, love letters, wedding invitations, family china—all these

FAMILY GROUP SHEET OF THE _____ FAMILY

	Source #			Source #

Full Name of Husband

His Father

His Mother with Maiden Name

Birth Date and Place

Marriage Date and Place

Death Date and Place

Burial

Full Name of Wife

Her Father

Her Mother with Maiden Name

Birth Date and Place

Death Date and Place

Burial

Other Spouses		Marriage Date and Place	

Children of This Marriage	Birth Date and Place	Death Date, Place and Burial	Marriage Date, Place and Spouse

things may be hiding in the attic or the basement of the subject's house. Ask permission to go fishing around there. You can learn a lot about the personalities of your subject's parents and siblings by looking at their belongings. Your subject, too, may become easier to understand after the two of you have looked at an old keepsake together. I'll never forget hearing Grandma's story of a ridiculous fight in 1948 with her soon-to-be ex-husband over who would get to keep a teapot planter after the divorce. She still has the teapot and took it down off the shelf to show me one day. It was not the object itself, but the look on her face as she held it out that I particularly enjoyed seeing. Beware: Rooting through attics can turn into a major endeavor if you're not careful.

Salt Lake City

The Church of Jesus Christ of Latter-day Saints, known as the Mormon Church, has the largest and best-organized collection of genealogical data on the planet. Mormon researchers have spent more than a century scouring courthouses, town halls, state agencies, church rosters, royal documents, town halls, and cemeteries in 110 countries to amass a genealogical database without peer: Over 750 million names of the deceased are now on file.

This is all because the Church believes in the doctrine of "baptism for the dead." It works like this: A living person, who must be a faithful Mormon, may have themselves re-baptized in a special church chamber in the name of a non-Mormon ancestor, who is then contacted by the angels in the hereafter and asked if they would like to accept this baptism by proxy. If the deceased agrees, they will enjoy a higher level of heaven. (In Mormon theology, almost everyone goes to one of many ascending layers of heaven.) The target need not be a blood relative: There have been proxy baptisms in the names of former U.S. presidents, monarchs of England, victims of historic tragedies, and famous writers and artists.

You don't have to be interested in converting to the Mormon Church to use their splendid database free of charge. The very best place to do this is at the Family History Library at 35 North Temple Street in Salt Lake City. The researchers there are friendly and helpful and will help you navigate the center's mammoth collection of 2.4 million rolls of microfilm, 310,000 books, and 700 computerized databases. Like attics, this place can be addictive, so plan to spend a few days. The Church also has smaller Family History Centers located in all fifty states. A list of these centers and their addresses can be found at familysearch.org. The Church also operates an online genealogical search tool at the same Web site, but far more information is available at the centers themselves, and, of course, at the granddaddy of them all out in Utah.

Other Libraries

Every state in the country has a library attached to its capitol's campus and these often contain rich lodes of vital statistics. This can be a great place to fill in missing names and dates on your Pedigree Chart. City and county libraries can also be a resource; they sometimes have genealogical sections of their own. At the very least, they'll have local newspapers indexed on microfilm. How about looking up your great-grandfather's wedding announcement or obituary? If the library is inadequate, try going to the newspaper's offices and asking to browse their morgue of past editions.

I did this at *The Arizona Republic*—where I worked as a reporter for a little over two years—to locate news clippings about the death of my great-uncle Warren LaRue, an important figure in my grandmother's life, who worked as a deputy sheriff and was killed in the line of duty with his partner in a Phoenix trailer park on January 18, 1971, two months before he was supposed to retire. I learned new details about what had happened to him and it was good to talk it over with my grandmother again. That same year, she and I and my uncle Fred attended an official Maricopa County Sheriff's Department memorial for fallen deputies. Fred is a jocular guy and not prone to making earnest statements, but after the event, he turned to me and said quietly, "You would have liked Warren." This was a haiku full of emotion for him.

County and state historical societies can also be good sources of data, but I've found them to be inconsistent in terms of quality. Some seem dedicated to archiving the work of the local amateur genealogists and tell you almost nothing about the actual history of the place. However, some gems can still be found in the files.

Two other libraries deserve mention. The New England Historic Genealogical Society, at 101 Newberry Street in Boston, has a superb collection of manuscripts and more than 200,000 books and periodicals. Their online catalog may be browsed at www.newenglandancestors.org. And the Allen County Public Library, in Fort Wayne, Indiana, has made it a special mission to acquire family histories from all over, plus registers of population going back to the American Revolution, as well a near-complete list of Civil War soldiers and widows. See what else they have at www.acpl.lib.in.us.

Courthouses

The American essayist Joan Didion once said that if you really want to take the temperature of life inside a major city, all you need to do is sit in the public gallery of the criminal court building and listen as the daily parade of the arrested is brought before the judge. This insight applies also to genealogy. Courtrooms can give you a view like none other onto the human condition in a given place and era. If you have the time and the patience, visit the county seat of the place where you know a particular ancestor once lived, and search the civil and criminal files for his name. This might yield nothing (our ancestors had the same motivations for avoiding courtroom dramas as we do) but you could also stumble upon some surprises if you're lucky.

Let's face it: Family trees can make for some awfully dull reading. We might be able to trace our lineage back ten generations, but we often know nothing about who these people actually *were*. Even basic details such as their appearance or their occupation is lost, let alone the fascinating trivia of their daily existence: the color of a favorite coat, a poem they may have written, the name of the family dog (and the brand of beer they favored). Courthouse proceedings might not provide all of that, but they can add a dose of color to otherwise dry recants.

Here's an example: My paternal grandfather's brother, a hardware merchant named Leslie Zoellner, spent years tracing back his descendants, some of whom had emigrated to northeastern Kansas from German farms in the 1840s. Other branches of the family apparently hit North American soil earlier. Leslie's hobby was tracking down all these people. Some folks collect coins or butterflies; Leslie collected his own bloodlines. He logged all the information by

hand into a series of bound volumes that read like a narrative diary. I'm not sure where Leslie got the following tidbit,
but it has the flavor of something uncovered in a dusty New
England courthouse registry and makes for a good tale, albeit one that raises more questions than it answers:

> William Sutton first appears at Barnstable on Cape
> Cod, where on 5 June 1666, he was hauled to court and
> fined for purloining the Bible from the meeting house,
> "one pound, and for telling a lye about the same, ten
> shillings." His departure from the town was probably
> expedited by the occurrences, and a few weeks later at
> neighboring settlement of Eastham, he took refuge in
> matrimony with Damaris Bishop.

That's my people: midnight moves and quickie marriages. So much more fun (and multidimensional) than
bare-bones names and dates.

Ellis Island

If one of your subjects' ancestors was among the great wave
of 22 million tempest-tossed that came to the United States
between 1890 and 1924, you'll want to visit ellisisland.org,
which posts passenger manifests of many of the ships that
docked at New York's port of entry for immigrants. On this
Web site you can find names, birthdays, occupations, home
countries, basic physical descriptions, and other information.

Genealogical and Family Societies

There is an army of hobbyist genealogists out there who
like nothing better than to compare their sources and look

for new ways to find old property deeds, marriage licenses, company reports, and the like. They maintain clubs and e-mail lists with names such as "The Northwest Pennsylvania Genealogical Society" or "The Descendants of John Harvey Jones." They often hold regular meetings and publish quarterly newsletters. You can find one that covers your area simply by running the words "genealogical society" plus your city or state through a search engine. A large list of them can also be found on rootsweb.com, or at http://www.familyhis tory.com/societyhall.

Online Resources

The Internet has completely transformed the science of genealogy, if only because it makes it that much easier for enterprising family detectives to find each other. You may find that the most valuable research actually comes from family trees and charts that others have gathered and passed along. Amateur genealogists are famous for their generosity and willingness to share their findings. Here's a list of the top five most useful Web sites in this subculture:

> CYNDI'S LIST: This monument to tenacity is the creation of Edgewood, Washington, housewife Cyndi Howells, who started keeping online bookmarks for her local genealogical society in 1996. The site has since become the premier "card catalog" for family heritage resources and receives up to 3 million hits a day. (www.cyndis list.com)

> ANCESTRY: Thousands of family trees are uploaded to this site but you must subscribe for a fee of approximately $30 per month to get full access to its resources.

Free articles and tipsheets are available, as well as some active message boards. (www.ancestry.com)

GENEALOGY: The other big pay-per-use site allows you to create a personal homepage with your genealogical data where it can be viewed by others. There's also a "virtual cemetery" where members have posted photos of their ancestor's grave markers. (www.genealogy.com)

FAMILY TOOLBOX: Similar to Cyndi's List, it also presents a multitude of genealogical sites in a searchable fashion. Also known as Helm's Genealogical Toolbox and publisher of the *Journal of Online Genealogy*. (www.familytoolbox.net)

HERITAGE QUEST: This publisher of genealogical books and reference materials also offers a great how-to primer on its Web site. (www.heritagequest.com)

Software

The tough job of keeping great-uncles from being mistaken for grandfathers in your notes has been made much easier by the advent of software that keeps all the lines straight. There are a number of excellent programs for sale in stores and online. Among the best are Family Tree Maker, Roots, and Family Matters. The Personal Ancestry File program is available as a free download from the Mormon Church at www.familysearch.org. The important thing to keep in mind when acquiring one of these programs is to make sure that it is compatible with the GEDCOM format. This is the standard language of genealogy programs, which will enable you to import data from other people's programs (and vice versa) via files with the suffix .ged. GEDCOM is a rough acronym for GEnealogical Data COMmunication, and the program ought to advertise this compatibility on its packaging.

MAKING A BOOK

You should now have a manuscript that runs anywhere from 10 to 200 pages, depending on how comprehensive you were in your conversations. You should store the document in a safety-deposit box, a metal filing cabinet, or some other place where it won't get lost or damaged. Make a photocopy as a backup. And then you should give strong consideration to turning your subject's story into a book.

What I did was both easy and cheap. I went down to my local photocopying shop—this one happened to be a Kinko's in downtown Phoenix—and asked the guys behind the counter how they created bound manuals for their business customers. All I had to do was to e-mail them the Microsoft Word file. I ordered five copies with paper covers and pages bound with black plastic spirals. This cost me about $70 and took about an afternoon to accomplish. I gave one copy to Grandma, one to each of her children, and kept two for myself. One of those copies sits on my bookshelf today.

Consider making your book even more durable and attractive by having it bound in hardcover. This is much easier and cheaper than it used to be, thanks to the advent of "print on demand" presses that use digital copying machines and advanced binding equipment to produce as many or as few books as the customer wants. This is a welcome step forward from the days of the vanity press, or self-publishing houses, some of which were known to charge authors unreasonably high fees for bulk shipments of their own books, often poorly designed and manufactured. Not all of these companies were bad, but many operated at the margins of respectability—alongside condo time-shares and mail-order vitamin supplements—preying on the writer's desperation to see their work published. Be careful when you select a self-publisher.

Here are three print-on-demand companies known to do reasonably good work:

LULU: This North Carolina company will allow you to upload your manuscript through their Web site and offers you a range of printing formats. Your biography can be bound with a spiral coil or more professionally bound like a regular hardback book with a photo of your choosing on the cover. You receive the finished product in the mail in about ten days. Cost per book ranges from $15 to $45. (Lulu.com)

BLURB: A high-quality printer that specializes in creating single copies of a hardback book of poetry, recipes, or photographs, with a Web-based feature that allows you to design a dust jacket and arrange the text on the page. Blurb can also, of course, print your biography. This would work especially well if you have a lot of photographs. Costs range from $30 to $80 per book, depending on page count. (Blurb.com)

iUNIVERSE: Founded in 1999, this company in Nebraska has a partnership with Barnes & Noble that allows self-published authors the chance to have their books displayed in a retail store and collect royalties (if they're lucky). Their model is different from the previous two. You must sign over your rights to the work. Paperback formatting starts at $299 and hardback at $499. You get ten free copies of your own book. (iuniverse.com)

VIDEO

Your subject's story is now down on paper. What about putting it on video? Creating a short home movie of your subject might be the best way to showcase the best stories they have to tell. You'll also have the pleasure of capturing their tics and mannerisms and laughter for future generations. Digital camcorders are easy to use, so you don't need to be Steven Spielberg to make a DVD of your subject talking to the camera for an hour.

Here are some quick tips to get the most out of the exercise. Much of the technical wisdom comes from Steve Pender, who has twenty-five years of experience in video production and now runs his own custom video company, Family Legacy Video, in Tucson, Arizona. Teri Duff, who runs Family Archive Films in Oakland, California, is also in the business of filming life-story interviews.

Go digital

If you don't already own a camcorder and plan to invest in one for this project, make it one that records in digital or on Mini-DV tapes. It will be much simpler to transfer your recording to a computer file and allows you to more easily update the format as technology evolves in the coming years. You'll also be able to move your film on the computer via the standard IEEE 1394 output (known as FireWire on the Macintosh and iLink on the PC). Video editing software now comes as standard equipment on many off-the-shelf computers, but if yours doesn't have it, good programs include Adobe Production Studio, Ulead VideoStudio, and Cyberlink PowerDirector. A camcorder will set you back anywhere from $280 to $600. Also make sure that it has a mount for a tripod at its base.

Pick the best stories

Your video will be much more entertaining if you can get your subject to go on at length about a topic close to their heart, instead of responding to a series of questions. By this point, you already know which stories are particularly apt to illuminate the subject's personality, mannerisms, and beliefs. Don't ask them to repeat basic family data, names or dates—that's what the written record is for. Instead, come prepared with a list of five really good anecdotes you'd like them to relate. Mix it up in terms of tone: Pick three serious stories and two funny ones that you know your subject can tell well. If you're having a hard time deciding, use this standard: Which stories do you want your own great-grandchildren to hear for themselves?

Prepare the room

Choose a pleasant and well-lit room. Don't go outside—the noise levels will likely be bad. Find a comfortable chair for the subject with something visually appealing in the background: a bookshelf, a wall full of art, a row of plants. Don't sit them in front of the drapes or worse, a white wall. It will look awful.

Sound test

Remember how you made triple-sure your cassette tape was actually recording good audio when you were doing the interviews? Do the same with the camcorder. Ask the subject to say their name and their birthday while you tape them. Make sure that the sounds of the air conditioner or the breeze from the window aren't obscuring your subject's words. Few things ruin an interview more than bad sound.

Mike them up

If you want to ensure top-quality sound, invest in a lavaliere microphone (about $120). You've seen these before—they're the small circular things clipped to the lapels of newscasters. The wire should connect to the audio port of your camcorder.

Still life

Gather together some important photographs from the subject's life and point the camera at them in extreme closeup before the interview begins. You can intersperse these into the video with the editing software, perhaps while the subject is talking in voice-over about the subject at hand, say, a photo of your grandma's late husband fills the screen when she talks about him, or a close shot of her high school diploma while she talks about graduation.

Light, more light

Bad lighting in the room can make your grandfather look sallow and half dead. Simply turning on the lights may not work because of the shadows. The best way to ensure that your subject looks bright and attractive, according to Steve Pender, is to use a three-point lighting system. You can re-create this Hollywood standard in the living room with a minimum of effort. Go to the local hardware store and buy three clamp lights, three 100-watt bulbs, a roll of duct tape, and three extension cords. Tape each light to a broom or a broomstick at a height of about three feet and then fasten the broomstick to a folding chair so it stands up by itself. Repeat this with the other two lamps. Then position one light behind the subject and away from the gaze of the cam-era. This is called the "back light." Aim one light directly at the subject. This is called the "key light." Aim the last one against a white wall so that the light bounces off from it and fills the room. That eliminates the shadows on the sub-ject's face and is called the "fill light." Plug all the lights in with the extension cords. Finally, sit yourself down in a comfortable chair facing the subject, at a distance of about three feet, and position the tripod-mounted camcorder over your shoulder and to your immediate right. You're ready to shoot.

Get comfortable

All the rules for your demeanor (see Chapter 3) are in effect, but even more so. Relax, have fun, and get the stories flow-ing. Your aim is to make the subject forget about the camera and the production preparations and simply be themselves as they recall what V-J Day was like in Seattle. Keep eye con-tact with them and encourage them to look at you, not the camera lens.

Record the silence

When you're ready to call it a day, be sure to record the silence of the room for about three minutes. This will give you some "sound patches" to plug into your edited video if you want to create a brief pause from one moment to the next. It will sound less choppy.

Talking to the professionals

If you don't feel comfortable shooting your own home video and want to outsource the job, there are a growing number of "personal historians" who have gone into business for the purpose of recording the life stories of older Americans. You can find one who lives near you though the Association of Personal Historians (www.personalhistorians.org), which has more than 500 members.

STORYCORPS

StoryCorps is one of the nation's most ambitious efforts to gather and preserve oral history. It consists of a series of mobile recording booths in which any ordinary person can reserve time and interview somebody close to them. For $10, you get an hour of time and a CD of your conversation. With your permission, the recording is donated to the Library of Congress where it will reside as long as there is a United States.

Grandchildren have interviewed grandparents, wives have interviewed husbands, and restaurant customers have interviewed their favorite waitresses. The stories, as you might imagine, are varied and colorful. Over the recording booths are the legends LISTENING IS AN ACT OF LOVE and LIS-TEN CLOSELY.

StoryCorps was founded by radio producer David Isay, who said he took his inspiration from the Works Progress Administration's Federal Writer's Project, which created work for a platoon of down-and-out authors during the Depression. These writers went out to the forgotten corners of the Midwest and the South and took interviews on primitive recording equipment with busted farmers, elderly former slaves, autoworkers, shopkeepers—the people who Walt Whitman called the "countless dissatisfied faces" of America. Economic times are better now, but the desire to share fragments of real life has not changed. Isay has said he hopes to accumulate a quarter million interviews of ordinary people in the next ten years.

After he helped dedicate the first StoryCorps booth in Grand Central Terminal in New York City, the eminent oral historian Studs Terkel looked up at the station's ceiling, decorated by an aquamarine map of the constellations, and remarked: "We know there's an architect, but who hung the iron? Who were the brick masons? Who swept the floors? They are the ones who make the world go around, those millions of people who have never expressed themselves."

That comes very close to the spirit behind this book, and the spirit behind all oral history. Find out about a StoryCorps booth in a city near you at www.storycorps.net.

Biography to Autobiography

If you've come this far with your subject, you don't need me to tell you about the most fascinating aspect of this project. You see it usually at a late stage, but it's as certain as a principle of physics, like the way that two parallel lines will appear to converge at a vanishing point on the horizon. Think of this as the optic law of biography: If you gaze into another's life long enough, you will inevitably see reflections of your own. The road out also leads in. And so if you've found yourself even more intrigued about your own past as a result of being somebody else's biographer, I encourage you to start writing your own life story. Don't wait for your own Boswell.

You can use exactly the same writing technique you've mastered for the first go-around. Ask yourself the same questions listed in Chapters 5 and 6. Consider also taking a trip back to places you lived before. Bring a notebook to jot down sights, sounds, and smells: physical sensation has a unique way of unlocking forgotten thoughts. Remember the power of the madeleine, the famous shell-shaped cake in Marcel Proust's *Remembrance of Things Past*. The narrator soaks a madeleine in linden tea, takes a bite, and suddenly experiences a jolt of sensory recall. He writes: "No sooner had the warm liquid, and the crumbs with it, touched my palate than a shudder ran through my whole body, and I stopped, intent upon the extraordinary changes that were taking place." You may be surprised what you find.

ANOTHER VIEW OF THE LIBRARY

However many of these documents you create, I hope you will consider donating at least one copy to your local library or historic society. They probably will be glad to keep it in their special collections. Five hundred years from now, your relative's life could provide key insights for someone on what things and people were like in this century. Your biography is a time traveler. Good stories should never die.

Two Brothers

When Max Forer started cleaning out some old desks in his button factory in New Jersey one day in the early 1990s, he found a stack of papers in a drawer. He immediately recognized the language as Yiddish, but he couldn't make any sense of them, except that they seemed to have been written by his grandfather Yosef in Poland before World War II. The letters had been stuck in the desk drawer and apparently forgotten for more than sixty years.

Max passed them on to his son, Howard, who paid to have them translated into English. And there Howard found a fascinating window into what life was like for his family immediately before the Nazi persecutions started in earnest. "The situation here by us is very bad and oppressive," wrote Yosef in one of the letters, dated August 20, 1939. "The fear of war hangs over our head! But we certainly have no need to be afraid because our needs are so small that whatever will be, let it be. And what will happen with everyone, will also be with us!"

Howard, then a forty-eight-year-old paralegal living in Glen Cove, New Jersey, was already in the middle of building a personal genealogy with the aid of a computer program called Family Tree Maker. He realized that the letters added a whole new dimension to that side of the family, and to Yosef in particular, but he wondered how to integrate them into his genealogy project. Then the solution came to him: Why not just upload the letters to an Internet site and let everybody in the family look at them?

Howard created a group site through MSN.com and posted everything he had found. Family members needed a password to access it, but once inside, they found a wealth of information. There were pictures of the four brothers who had emigrated from Poland, a massive family tree dating from 1855, translated copies of Yosef's desk-drawer letters, current pictures of descendants now living in nine different countries, and a message board. This last feature was to prove important, as Howard eventually heard from hundreds of people to whom he was related and who had found out about the Web site. Howard told me that this brought him immense satisfaction because his late father Max—the one who had given him the letters—had never known much about the pioneers of the family who had come to America to escape persecution.

"My father really wanted to connect with some of the branches of the family and wanted to find some of these people for his own satisfaction," he said. "I myself never knew who my family was. This gave me a way to unite people—with each other and with me. It's a way to leave something behind for my children."

His brother Eddie, a sales executive who lives in Manhattan, also used technology to help him understand more about his family. Like Howard, Eddie was interested in the specific memories of his ancestors, but he focused his attention on his mother's side of the family. And he, too, had a gift from the past. At some point in the late 1970s, his mother had the foresight to buy a battery-operated tape recorder from a department store and set it in front of her father, Herman, and her aunt, Rose.

As far as Eddie can tell, this conversation took place in the front yard of the family home in Fairlawn, New Jersey, because the sounds of cars backing in and out of the driveway can be clearly heard. Herman can also be heard complaining the whole time that he has no interest in talking about his life as a newsstand operator, but he never becomes irritated enough to get up and leave. Rose, meanwhile, tells a story about being sent over from Russia at the turn of the century, with only fifty cents in her pocket and the name of a relative written on a scrap of paper. She began work as a seamstress in a warehouse full of women who did nothing but sew clothes all day long, but Rose distinguished herself by learning how to fix the sewing machines when they broke. This allowed her a measure of prosperity.

There was only one copy of this cassette tape, which was also the only existing recording of Rose and Herman's voices. It was full of yard noise, with a lot of hissing and popping, and had become stretched by multiple playings. Eddie was afraid it might break, so he took it to an amateur musician friend of his in Chicago, who hooked up a tape deck to his computer (see Chapter 2 for details), saved the conversation as an MP3 file, and used an audio-quality program—such as SoundSoap or Magix—to clean up the extraneous noise. He then presented Eddie with a compact disc that contained a much more audible conversation. It will also last a lot longer than a tape.

10

A Final Thought

At the end of one evening, I got Grandma talking about a bicycle she owned when she was eight. The following sentence emerged. I think it is the most beautiful sentence I have ever encountered inside or outside of literature, and I expect that, long after she is gone, I will be reading it over and over (and, hopefully, those descendants of mine who never knew her will be reading it, too). I'll quote it entirely, just as she said it.

You don't realize now at all, of course, but there is an incline there from the Papago Buttes, the land does go down and I would get on my bicycle right where the turnoff is into the farm at the start of the lane and pump as hard as I could on my bicycle and see how far I could coast and the last part of it would be through the alfalfa and I can remember going along with the alfalfa in bloom and that is a really lovely smell and all the yellow butterflies all flying all over the blooms and back and

*forth and the sky real blue and white clouds and just this
exhilarating feeling of flying along on the bicycle and going through the butterflies and smelling the alfalfa and it
was a good, good feeling.*

This memory of a summer day in 1923 had been locked
inside Grandma's mind all this time: a small, unremarkable,
and utterly lovely image that comes close to the heart of
what it means to be young and alive. It might have remained
there—and died with her—if it hadn't been prompted out.

I don't know why this sentence makes me feel happy
every time I read it. Maybe it's because it poured out from
Grandma's mouth in an uncharacteristic rush of words. Or
maybe I've had times like that in my own ever-receding childhood and I know exactly what that day must have been like
for her. Or perhaps it was the feeling that a piece of her childhood had been given back to her for a minute, like Mildred
Baker's ball lost underneath the floorboards all those years.

Or maybe because I know I never would have heard
about it at all had we not been talking that evening.

Notes on Sources

The account of Mildred Baker's ball comes from "A Ball Lost for 78 Years is '91 Christmas Present," published in *The Smith County Pioneer*, January 2, 1992, and from the radio segment "Woman Recovers Toy Ball After 78 Years," hosted by Scott Simon on National Public Radio on January 11, 1992. The heritage of oral history gets a thorough analysis in *The Voice of the Past: Oral History*, by Paul Thompson (New York: Oxford University Press, 2000). Techniques and forms of oral history are discussed in *Like It Was: A Complete Guide to Writing Oral History*, by Cynthia Stokes Brown (New York: Teachers & Writers Collaborative, 1988). Kristin Gilger's story of her family was originally published by the Salem *Statesman Journal* and reprinted in the 1998 special section "Under the Influence." Lori Hope Lefkovitz's insightful essay "Inherited Holocaust Memory and the Ethics of Ventriloquism," was published in the winter 1997 edition of the *Kenyon Review*. The story of William Manchester's combat experience was taken from his autobiography *Goodbye, Darkness* (New York: Little, Brown, 1979). Excellent advice on nonfiction writing can be found in *The Art and Craft of Feature Writing*, by William

Blundell (New York: Plume, 1986). Some conversational styles are examined in *Interviews that Work: A Practical Guide for Journalists*, by Shirley Biagi (Belmont, CA: Wadsworth Publishing Company, 1992). Forms of biographical story-telling are discussed in *How to Write Your Own Life Story*, by Lois Daniel (Chicago: Chicago Review Press, 1997). Excellent writing tips can be found in *Writing Tools*, by Roy Peter Clark (New York: Little, Brown, 2006). Owen Lattimore's quote was taken from "Cultivating Loneliness," by Robert D. Kaplan in the *Columbia Journalism Review*, January/February 2006. Genealogical technique is explained in *Secrets of Tracing Your Ancestors*, by W. Daniel Qullien (Cold Spring Harbor, NY: Cold Spring Press, 2003). Tips on video production were drawn from the informative CD *Producer's Guide*, by Steve Pender (Tucson, AZ: Family Legacy Video, 2003). Studs Terkel's quote about the ceiling of Grand Central Terminal comes from the magazine article "Hear Here" (*Smithsonian*, June 2004).

Thanks to Kevin Gass, Martha Brantley,
and Jeanette Marquez-Durant
for valuable assistance.

This book is dedicated to
Ann Mary von Blume.